To. Jerry

With best wishes for
your Happiness in
Retirement.

William Barber
29 Nov '96

Love prefers twilight to daylight.
-- Oliver Wendell Holmes

The grand essentials of happiness are: something to do, something to love, and something to hope for.
-- Allan K. Chalmers

Happiness is not a destination. It is a method of life.
-- Burton Hills

RETIREMENT

... THE TIME FOR

REAL HAPPINESS

by

Walter O. Bachus

RETIREMENT — THE TIME FOR REAL HAPPINESS
a book published in-house by the Author

Library of Congress Catalogue Card Number: 96-94855

ISBN 0-9655395-0-4

Manufactured in the United States of America

*T*o my wife,

Helen --

my partner in life and my love,

forever.

ACKNOWLEDGMENT:

The cover photograph is from
Aris © Entertainment, 1991

CONTENTS

FOREWORD

W ILL you retire soon? Or, are you already retired and still looking for the right combination to find a happy retired life? Maybe you retired some time ago and now find that you need a change. Or, possibly, you are not retiring, but you have a friend or loved one who is retired or shortly will be. For all of you, this book should be a real blessing.

Today, people are living longer. Back in 1900, the average person could expect to live to the ripe old age of 47. By 1950, this figure had increased to 68. It continued to climb: by 1990, 79 for women, and 72 for men.[1] Then, by 1992, it stood at 76 (all sexes) and was projected to rise to 78 by year 2010.[2]

Longer life spans mean that our population will include greater numbers of people in the so-called "advancing years." For example, in 1992, our country had 32.3 million people in the 65-year or older category[3] — a whopping 12.5 percent of the total. Such demographics are found all over the world. Presently, more than 10 percent of the people, worldwide, are over the age of 65. This is a new record in our history books; America, and the world, are "graying" at an ever increasing speed. Retirement has become a reality for a growing number of our population. According to AARP (the American

Association of Retired Persons), only about 11% of the older Americans (those over 65) were in the labor force in 1993 (3.5 million of the 32.8 million older population). The rest of the older population -- 29.3 million, or 89% -- was retired.[4]

These retired folks also have more money to spend. Ask any marketeer! Back in 1970, 16% of the 65 plus years people were receiving retirement pensions from private pension plans; by 1989, the number climbed to 29%.[5]

Thus, there are growing numbers of older people, more in the retired category, more of those who have money to spend. For all of them, this should be the life for which they have been waiting: the so-called "Golden Years." However, the sad fact is that many of these retired people are *not* really happy or satisfied. They are a long way from truly enjoying life. Worse still, they have no idea of how to go about changing the course of events. Many feel utterly "stranded."

This book is designed to help prospective retirees and those recently retired to quickly and easily find happiness in retirement. For the past 17 years, my occupation and personal experience have given me unique opportunities to observe and work with large numbers of retired people. Moreover, I, myself, retired more than three years ago. I can truly report that I enjoy every minute of every day. I believe that I now know the secrets of finding a happy retired life. I am also quite sure that I can share these secrets with you. As examples or models, I will be using my own experiences and those of my wife. To our own personal experiences, I will add the countless, documented observations of others, often sharing quotations from some of the "experts." I will show you in simple, understandable language why some people can so easily find happiness in retirement and why others do not.

In this book, I will carefully show you how to

"discover" the many, many things in retired life that you would really be happy doing. Then, with your new discoveries, you will learn how to design your very own Personal Retirement Plan. Your plan will be uniquely suited to your own tastes, likes, and desires. You will quickly see that your unique plan is designed to deliver satisfaction each day of the year -- with no boredom, ever. You will also see that these happy days can continue for the rest of your life.

By reading this book, you will discover ways to share your newly found happiness with others. Sharing with friends and loved ones is always something special. Well, how about it? Does it sound interesting? Promising? Well, it should. As you read, remember that I am speaking to you as a fellow retired person. Speaking from experience, I know the real happiness that retired life can really bring and how to go about finding it.

Like many of my cohorts, and probably, yours, I enjoyed working and experienced a measure of success. I spent extended, hard hours at the office. Sometimes I longed for more time with my family, but that rarely occurred. Now, in retirement, I am having the time of my life. They will never see me back at work. *I have found the life to live.* So, to those of you who recently retired, and to you who soon will, I say: "Come on in. The water's fine!"

In spite of the joy one can find in retirement, for many people, there remain many misconceptions about what to expect in retired life. I find a lot of the people really do not expect much from retirement. Worse yet, a conversation with them shows that they do not know how to go about finding true happiness after they leave the work force.

For instance, right after I retired, many of my friends couldn't wait to ask me what I found to do in retirement. They were sure I was quite miserable. Some of them would say: "I can't believe you are retired. What do you do now with all your time?" Others would snuggle up to me at a party and whisper: "You were always so fully engaged at work, may I ask you how you spend your day now that you are retired?" Many would add their favorite question: "Don't you get bored and wish you were back at work?"

Ah, but they were missing something and failing to see that there is an opposite horizon out there. Even before I retired, I saw lots of bumper stickers, that although intended to be humorous, were revealing. You've probably seen some too. One said: "Retired -- No Work -- No Pay -- BUT -- No Worries!" Another read: "Retired and Enjoying Life (Finally)." And one which particularly tickles me a little proclaimed: "Retired and Spending My Children's Inheritance!" So, I suspected that there was a lot of unexperienced joy out there somewhere; it was my job to find it.

Those friends who asked me what I was finding to do to stay busy and wondering, confidentially, if I were not a little bored, were overlooking two things:

1) They did not know that I'd never been happier, *or busier*. Once I retired, there was not a spare moment for anything that was not carefully planned. No matter how hard I tried to convince these Doubting Thomases that these were, indeed, the Golden Years, they found it really hard to believe.

2) These skeptical friends were silently venting some of their *own* personal fears and frustrations. They knew that they, too, would someday retire. They were silently fearing that day. They didn't want to be bored, and they were afraid that they would have too much time on their hands with nothing to do. They also suspected that being disengaged from the work force would push them into a non-productive, unsatisfying, and often insecure life. They simply did not

know if they would be able to handle it. Worse still, many really believed the frightening tale that we hear time and time again -- that tale which says: "Once a person retires, if he doesn't quickly become engaged again in something meaningful (maybe even a new job), then, that person won't live very long." That one really grabs them. This type of thinking seems in keeping with the general belief that many people rapidly decline after retiring. Some will go on to recite several personal experiences to make their point.

What underlies these general attitudes? The answer could well be fear -- fear of the unknown (which most of us know and understand) and fear that retirement will bring all the bad things of life, including boredom and old age. Such beliefs need to be heartily challenged, and they will be in this book. Together, we will subject each of these attitudes and beliefs to close scrutiny. We will learn how to replace any attendant unhealthy, negative thoughts that may have rubbed off with positive, reinforcing concepts. This will arm us to explore the bright prospects of the future.

For those of you who have not yet left the work force but are on the brink of retirement, this book is made to order. I've caught you in time to help you avoid some of the pitfalls that many retirees experience. I would add to this group those who are recent retirees and are not yet into a rut. You, too, can learn how to start right away and find true happiness in retirement. You will quickly discover that this book is loaded with practical suggestions and logical steps to take.

You cannot start thinking about retirement too early. You need to give a lot of thought to the kinds of things you always wanted to do but for which you could never find the time while working. I want to suggest some of the ways you might think about these important things. In addition, I will show you how to make time your best *ally*, not your enemy.

This book will help you build the right foundation for your own happy days in retirement.

For others of you who are already retired but are not really happy -- even for those who may be experiencing a little happiness along the way, but not enough -- this book is for you, too. You will quickly find that it is not too late to change your pattern and find new horizons. You can easily get out of your ruts. I will help you rechart your course, offering you practical suggestions, guides, examples, and descriptive programs. I know that if you try them, you will like your new retired life.

The final portions of the book are directed at making your joy filled days last. What's the good of having fun if it has to end too soon? As we will see, it doesn't have to end! Moreover, as mentioned earlier, you will learn how to share this "good news" with others -- a special treat. Finally, I'll give you a few bonus suggestions and special hints for a happy retirement. This will include going over a few typical schedules of my own "live" retirement days, weeks, and months. You will see that these are based on my own personal retirement plan and the happy days I have experienced.

Several of my closest friends and I have thoroughly tried and tested everything that you will read about in this book. These strategies work! As you might expect, some of the things that I sampled right after retiring have been modified or improved. If I were to retire tomorrow, I still might do things a bit differently than I did several years ago. Nonetheless, I'd most certainly follow the solid suggestions offered in this book. Having tried and refined them myself, then tested them on my friends, I know they work.

To you, the reader, I say: "Happy retirement planning!" You are on the threshold of the best days of your life. This book will show you how.

PREFACE

a word or two about the author who has found real happiness in retirement

BEFORE we start, let's get a little better acquainted. I am a native of Tyler, Texas, having received my Bachelor of Science degree in Civil Engineering from Texas A&M University in 1950. Later, in 1957 at New York University, I graduated with a Master of Science degree in Industrial Engineering. I also am a graduate of the Harvard Business School and several Army schools and universities. These include the Army's Engineer School, The Command and General Staff College, The Armed Forces Staff College, and the Army War College.

After graduating from college in 1950, the Army dispatched all of us green second lieutenants to Korea, where the war had just started. I found that I liked Army life, and I served as a regular officer in the Corps of Engineers for 28 years. I progressed "through the ranks," as they say, holding many command and staff positions in Europe, Japan, Korea, and Vietnam. I retired from the Army in 1978 as a Brigadier General.

My first retirement was short lived. Within five days, I accepted employment as the Executive Director of The Society of American Military Engineers. This is a professional engineer society. An urgent vacancy occurred, and the governing Board wanted me. There, I served as the Chief Operating Officer for nearly fifteen years, fully retiring in May 1993.

Much earlier, in Europe right after World War II, I met my dear wife, Helen. Although she hailed initially from Vienna, Austria, she lived most of the war-years in London, England with her mother and sister. Married nearly 50 years ago, my wife and I have two children. Both are married and live nearby. Helen and I also have four grandchildren. We presently reside in Alexandria, Virginia and own a vacation condo right on the beach in Ocean City, Maryland.

I hope this does not seem self-centered; my purpose in sketching these facts is to put us on a more congenial footing so that I may speak as your "friend," as the book proceeds. I wish it were possible for me to read your biography too. My main hope, however, continues to be that I can somehow find the right words and thoughts to convey the genuine happiness that my wife and I are experiencing in retirement, clearly sharing with you how we went about finding it. We sincerely believe that we can help you find real happiness in your retirement too. We know it's out there for us all.

1

ARE RETIRED PEOPLE HAPPY?

L ET me ask you how many *happy retired people* you know. Careful now! How many do you know who are *truly* happy? Would you say that most of them are happy? If you really know them, perhaps you would say that this appearance of happiness just a facade. Have their advanced years enabled them to put up a pretty good front? When you take time and get close to them, do they start to confide that retirement is really not all they had expected?

I must confess that this is a loaded question. Upon retirement, most people seem to exhibit great, nearly euphoric, joy. They feel like the weight of the world has been lifted from their shoulders. We've all seen them. After a relatively short period, however, if these people do not engage themselves in a satisfying and stable retirement life, they find themselves slipping into a prolonged period of disenchantment. This is the reason why many retired people seem less than happy. Many are downright unhappy.

Upon closer observation, most of the retired

community will admit that they are simply bored to one degree or another. Their retired days just seem to bring a lot of monotony. Their activities simply do not bring real satisfaction. They find that time -- which, perhaps, was formerly their worst enemy -- is still not a friend. Now time just strings out the day.

Some of the retired people I know wish they were still back at work. They would like to be engaged in what they call, "meaningful things" -- activities that would bring daily rewards and restful nights. Some also miss their comrades back in the office. They wonder how things are going "back there" without them.

Furthermore, a lot of retired people understandably link retirement with the aging process. The two seem to go hand-in-hand. Some also accept the premise that the aging human machine must undergo aches and pains and will naturally experience less happiness and satisfaction as the years roll on.

These observations are rather common, if you really probe deeply into the psyche of retired people. If you are retired, or will be shortly, you might be a little alarmed and definitely concerned. I certainly was right after I retired. True, my immediate past employment kept me in constant contact with large numbers of retired people. Part of my job was to counsel retired military officers -- to help them transition into civilian life. This involved helping place them in new jobs and eventually working with those who would fully retire. I did this for nearly 15 years. During this time, I also frequently visited three large retirement centers in the local area. There I worked closely with other large groups of retirees, many of whom were advancing in years.

I thought I knew and understood retirement, with all of its problems and its promises. Yet, I found, after retiring, that retired life for many was even worse than I thought. To be sure that what I was seeing and observing in my fellow retired friends was an accurate picture, I conducted some pretty intensive investigations and studies. I used the many parties and socials, along with my numerous visits to the nearby retirement centers, to gather the evidence. I made it a special point to randomly discuss state of mind and degree of happiness with as many people as I could. I kept notes and carefully developed and documented correlations and trends.

These discussions with my retired friends were far from being formal interviews, in the strict sense. To the contrary, they were low-key conversations which I enjoyed during the normal course of events with my friends. In retrospect, I am sure they did not even know (or suspect) that they were being interviewed. Informal as these sessions were, however, I sometimes probed deeply to see how my retired friends really felt about certain key elements, such as:

1. Do you miss working?
2. Do you miss the people back at work?
3. Did you wish you, yourself, were working again?
4. How busy are you now, in retirement?
5. Do you ever find that you get bored?
6. Do you have enough to do now? Does time seem to drag?
7. Would you like to find other interesting things to do? Are you looking?
8. Do you now generally enjoy your friends and associates?
9. Are you satisfied with your retired life at present?
10. Would you say that you are truly "happy?"

11. How long have you been retired?
12. How is your health? Any specific problems?
13. Are you married and living with your spouse?
14. If your spouse has passed on, how has your life changed as a result?

At one point I even developed a formal questionnaire along the lines of the above questions. But when I studied the data I had already gathered, I wasn't too sure that any of the "new" answers from the questionnaires would be much different from those already gathered informally, in face-to-face conversations. For that reason, I dropped the formal questionnaire idea.

I continued to play the little game of asking a lot of questions during large gatherings and at socials, listening and watching carefully. My friends did not seem to mind. I guess all people like to talk about themselves.

Sometimes, as the informal interview process continued, it was necessary to meet privately with one or two of the people I saw in larger groups. I wanted to be sure that I clearly understood their answers. I usually invited my friend (or friends) over for a snack (or, with luck, got invited over to their house).

So it went with the data gathering phase. I continued with these in-depth probes and face-to-face discussions up to the point where the data seemed to be confirmed, that is, when the answers began to be repeated.

Finally, it was decision time. What did all the data collection and data compiling reveal? On the first three questions (about working), I found that *most* of the *recent* retirees (those retired less than two years), definitely missed work and their work mates. Nearly half seemed ready to go back to work. Half is a lot! Remember, these were people who were supposed to be enjoying their Golden Years.

On the next four questions -- what they were doing with their retired lives, if they had enough to do (i.e., were they busy?), and the degree of boredom experienced -- I found that *well over half* really would like to find other things to do. They had too much repetition in their lives. They were, plainly, getting into the proverbial rut. However, it seemed they needed a lot of coaxing to move them toward new activities. They definitely seemed short on ideas. Although most of them had friends with varied activities, they, themselves, just seemed to lack the enthusiasm or energy to dig in and find new things. This same group, almost without exception, admitted that at times they were a little bored.

As to the degree of satisfaction and happiness being experienced in retirement, the *large majority* quickly indicated they were, indeed, happy. Yet, with additional probing and jumping back and forth between "yesterday" and "today," -- making comparisons between the two -- the picture gradually changed. It became more and more apparent that they had some *major reservations* about how they viewed their lives. It would be fair to say that *at least half*, were "not sure." Of course, they would like to have everybody think that they were *very* happy and satisfied -- nobody really likes a "griper" -- but you could see by their body language and facial expressions that they had experienced happier days in the past. Not only this, but the large majority seemed to express major doubts and uncertainties about the future. This compounded their inability to express total satisfaction with their retired lives and what tomorrow held.

During the final phases, I wanted to very gently determine if the friend being questioned had any extreme health problems. Being healthy and well seems to mean so very much to us all -- especially to the aging. Here freedom from aches and pains gives one a new perspective and better outlook.

I managed to confirm their marital status and the details of their marriage. The folks without spouses naturally had different lives than the married ones with living spouses. In addition, I tried to catalogue the friend by how long he (or she) had been retired. This seemed to clarify the outlook of the two groups -- those recently retired and those who retired several years earlier. This information seemed to sharpen up the conclusions, but did not really influence the results much. The folks with longer tenure of retirement were either resigned to things (good or bad), or they were even more restless. They, too, however, were wide open for suggestions.

One thing is certain from my investigations: there are *a lot* of unhappy retired people out there, folks who are definitely not enjoying life to the fullest. They welcome suggestions about how to change their lives for the better. While only a few seemed "desperate," there were sizable numbers who were ready and eager for new directions.

2

CAN RETIREMENT BRING HAPPINESS?

S TARTING with the premise that many retired people are not truly happy or satisfied leads us to a key question: *What do we really mean by* happiness? The best way to find the answers is to analyze the various components of happiness: what it takes to make a person truly happy. This brief analysis should give us the proper tools to search for happiness -- anywhere, anytime. It should also help us find out why people are not so happy with their retired lives and what is lacking.

After digging deeply into the meaning of happiness, we'll take a closer look at "old age." We'll review why we already have some definite mind sets about aging. We'll see why many of our present attitudes are real obstacles to living happy lives as seniors. Next, we'll take a similar look at retirement to see how we are conditioned to expect the worst from it -- ours or anybody's. Then, we'll link both aging and retirement and see how the composite picture of retiring and being old, too, is really "bad news." If we had to stop at that point, we might rightly conclude that it is nearly impossible for a retired person in advancing years to think that he has any chance of being happy.

Ah, but, the "good news" follows. We will take a careful look at the opposite end of the spectrum. We'll study a different set of seniors who, although retired and getting older, too, are having the time of their lives. Our task will be to find out how they did it and why, because, as we will learn, if a few can get old, retire, and be very happy, that means that many (perhaps all of us) can, too. We will follow this by testing retired life from several different angles. This will enable us to correctly conclude, together, that retirement *can* meet all the tests of delivering true happiness.

The objective of our initial studies, then, is to assure that we are absolutely convinced that *anybody* can find happiness -- anytime -- in retirement as well. We do not want to have any doubts or reservations about this important point.

What is Happiness?

To begin, let's see if we can get some pretty good understanding and agreement on what it means to be really happy. This will provide us a convenient way to gauge our expectations of retired life and to see whether it will really be able to deliver all that we want it to.

We know that, being human, everybody experiences some happy days and some days which are not so happy. Also, our associations with others teach us that some people are happy most of the time. We would be correct in categorizing -- labeling -- such people as "happy people." Of course, some people would never seem to be able to fit this mold. Some, in fact; are unhappy most of the time. Still, with all our experience in living with people and observing them -- the happy ones and the others -- we might have difficulty in answering the question, "What is happiness?"

We pretty well know when we are happy and when we are not. We also know when we are looking at a happy person and one who isn't. But what makes a person (or ourselves) really happy -- or sad? While you are thinking about this question and grasping for answers (and I hope you are), let me briefly share what some of the "experts" say.

In reviewing many sources, I found that experts have widely varying opinions on what creates happiness. However, on close examination, most experts seem to agree on certain elements. Included are the following: inner peace; freedom from want, fear and pain; general satisfaction; a feeling of worth (or value); being respected; and being loved.

My own favorite list comes from Norman Vincent Peale. He calls them: "...the components of happiness" -- or "the Happiness Mix." He lists them as follows: 1) spiritual experience, 2) deep inner peace, 3) serenity, 4) joy, 5) excitement, 6) struggle, 7) good digestion, 8) health, 9) someone to love, 10) someone to love you, and 11) enough money for expenses.[6]

If you carefully look at Dr. Peale's list, you should be able to spot nearly every major component you can think of. All others, I believe, would be a subset of one of Dr. Peale's eleven components. For example, let's consider just a few of the key ingredients from Dr. Peale's list. Let's say that a person has deep inner peace, serenity, joy, excitement, love, and enough money for expenses. For that person, wouldn't it be fair to say that he (or she) is on the brink of happiness? It certainly seems so.

So, for now, let's go with Dr. Peale's list. We'll return to the various components later in the text.

How Do We View "Old Age?"

I should warn the reader at the start of this section that our early discussions about aging are likely to be a little sad, even dismal. We'll be looking at the "real world" we think we see. You might find yourself getting into a gloomy mood as we proceed with our discussions. As you continue, this might seem a bit puzzling, since you probably already expected that the main thrust of the book would be very positive. Before we get to that point, however, I must ask the reader to look at the other side. You will be comforted to know that the process is designed, ultimately, to leave you happy and satisfied and in the right frame of mind for the future.

The best way to start, I believe, is to be sure that we understand *how* and *why* we have certain attitudes about aging (and even retirement). After brief glimpses of one side of the coin, we'll quickly flip to the other -- both sides coming from our so-called "real world." First, we will explore what most people (including us) think they see, due to what they've learned and been conditioned to perceive. Then, almost without notice, we'll jump to the opposite coin side examine the "opposite view." Once we are sure we see the happy people on this other side, we'll also learn how to keep these right pictures in our consciousness. With that procedure in mind, let's struggle a little together with the promise that better things lie ahead.

Let's turn, then, to looking at how most people view "old age" -- the ripened years. As we all know, they are commonly called the "Golden Years." This means, of course, that the advanced years are supposed to be "golden" -- happy. However, when we consider how *most of us* look at old age, and the aging process, we realize that we probably expect that our old age will bring us anything but happy times. They certainly don't seem to have much prospect for being "golden." In fact, we probably expect "the worst."

Why is this? We all "know" what we are "seeing" and what we are "learning" from our observations of "old people." These observations start from youth and continue to present, and they teach us many lessons, some of them indelibly written in our minds. Many of us may now firmly believe that old age brings anything but joy.

To make this point a little clearer, let's ask ourselves what we "see" when we watch a group of older people. Let's make this a group of *very* old people, maybe in a nursing home. As we watch these older folks, it would not be unusual to see a lot of strange looking paraphernalia, and aids sitting around or in use. All of these things are designed to help our seniors. Here, we're speaking of things and devices like eye glasses, hearing aids, false teeth, walking canes, walkers, and wheelchairs. Viewed individually we don't pay them much attention. But, when we see a whole room or a place cluttered up with such devices -- again, a place like the nursing home -- they do get our attention. We might not be too comfortable around them, either, unless we have needed the assistance that these devices can provide, or have been around them long enough to get used to them.

When we are around these types of things, we try to overlook them. We certainly don't mean to embarrass the wearer, or user, but it is hard to look on them as being commonplace. Younger people would view some of these devices with even more alarm.

As we visit with our older people, aside from the devices and things that we see being used, the people themselves would tell us a lot. They would not have to say much of anything, but the messages would seem clear. We would notice a case here -- a case there: We'd witness poor eyesight, difficulty in hearing, occasional immobility, and maybe, other problems as well. No doubt about the message here: the human bodies of our seniors are going down hill. To a lesser extent, perhaps, we might also sometimes observe an occasional mental lapse, a mental breakdown, or even more frequently, short memories. Not only the body, but the mind is also wearing!

If we listen in on the conversations of our elders, we might also be even more dismayed. Our eavesdropping would confirm that we were hearing discussions monopolized by stories of declining health, sickness, slow recovery, and a lot of other unhappy events and experiences. These conversations might dominate most discussions. Sometimes as we are listening, we might remember that the bad news we thought we saw before in our older people -- the slide downhill because of physical and mental conditions -- suddenly seems to be compounded. The thoughts and minds of our older people are preoccupied with sad stories and reports.

So far, we've been talking about our own observations of aging -- what we, ourselves, see, hear, and observe. These may seem bad enough, but to round out our own learning experience, we must also add the stories and "lessons" we hear from others along the way. As if we had not ourselves seen and heard enough, we get a generous sprinkling of bad news from our friends, loved ones, and acquaintances.

From early childhood we listened to story after story about the glow and beauty of youth, and the ugliness and pity of old age. Sometimes these stories were relayed by those we trusted and respected -- our parents, teachers, and others in positions of great admiration. At other times it might have been a friend telling a joke or funny story about some *old guy* or *old dame*. Looking back, maybe now these jokes and stories are not so funny, but since these stories came from our friends and loved ones, they have taken on great credibility. Why -- or how -- then, could we believe otherwise?

The sad bottom line to our own observations, corroborated by the stories we heard and the lessons we learned, is that old age is something really bad. We know that it is coming, and we don't like it. Like frightened children, we might like to turn and run from it if we could, but we can't. We seem to be stuck with it!

Hold on a minute. Let's not get too bogged down with these experiences of remorse. At the outset you were promised brighter days are ahead. We will shortly see (and I hope remember) that there are some important exceptions to aging, to the gloomy observations and stories that we have seen and heard. There is an opposite side of the coin. When we get to these exceptions, they will bring real relief and offer great hope. I promise!

Viewing Retirement

Retirement should mean freedom -- freedom from the work routine, freedom to find and enjoy the things in life that a person really wants to do. Retirement should also be expected to bring more time -- time to enjoy what we find pleasant and good. This includes having more time to spend with our family and friends. Moreover, it should provide us more time to take care of ourselves, physically, mentally, and spiritually.

If this is so, shouldn't we really be looking forward to retiring? Maybe we should, viewed from this perspective, but, unfortunately -- as with our notions about old age -- our minds are already jammed with *different lessons*.

For example, let's take some of the false lessons about working. Through a gradual and deliberate process, we are led to believe that the only *really* happy people are those who work hard every day and achieve miracles. We are taught to accept and admire a hard worker, an achiever, and we should. We all are encouraged from a very early age to get into that mold and succeed. We are taught that, to survive and do well, we must jump into the same pattern.

We also are taught that hard work brings great personal rewards. Some of these are financial, bringing security and a good standard of living. Some are non-monetary and psychological, like self esteem and recognition. Most of these have great appeal to one's inner self. Often, we are taught that these non-monetary rewards are *the* most vital and can be fulfilled only by success at work. The message (both financial and non-financial) is this: "Never quit work!"

It naturally seems to follow that if a person is working hard (and often long), accomplishing a lot, and influencing the course of world events, that person is destined to be happy. On top of all of this, the hardworking person should also have the deep personal satisfaction that success and hard work bring. Our observations tend to confirm this most of the time; don't they? If this is the case, then what happens to a person when this work process stops? It is like the giant machine of progress coming to a screeching halt!

It just seems so normal, then, that after being heavily and happily immersed in the work mold, an abrupt end to it means not only that our work has stopped, but also that our happiness has ceased. It seems so logical and in keeping with all that we see and know. While we were out there working hard, we were happy. Now that we are idle, we can no longer be happy. One follows the other. It makes absolutely no sense that, once retired, we could continue to enjoy ourselves or to be very happy. If we could, it would be utterly contrary to our conditioning and learning for so many years.

Do you see anything alarming or upsetting about our

conclusions and the "lessons" learned? Without knowing it, and certainly without intending to do so, we just bought an attitude that will promote an unhappy retirement, no matter what we do. Maybe our frame of mind will also net us a little boredom to boot -- great! Just what we needed in retirement, a boring life on top of it all.

Ah, but again -- watch for that opposite side of the coin. What we've been seeing and hearing, and what we've been conditioned and educated into accepting, must now be "unlearned." We must now work to learn, and know, that this new retired life of ours *can* deliver satisfaction and meet each one of our individual needs and desires, just as well as our work life did -- for some, even more so.

At this point, like our discussions on aging, our grounds for optimism might not make much sense, but the basis for hope will become clearer. It should already sound obvious that it will be easier to find happiness in retired life if we think we have a chance of doing so. As with aging, I ask you to bear with me for the moment. The case will be completely clear shortly, very shortly.

The "Link" Between Old Age and Retirement

At a certain point in life, we seem to accumulate sufficient years to retire. If we were playing an imaginary game called "Retirement," we might view these years as points on our game scoreboard. In order to "win" -- to retire -- we have to score sufficient points (years).

Statistically, in real life, this retirement win seems to be somewhere around 60 plus years, maybe 65, or even 70; sometimes it is even a little older. Of course, some people retire earlier, for various reasons, some later, and some (sadly) will never retire.[7] We hear common reports that the retirement age drops every year. That is undoubtedly true.

However, it seems to be a given that for one to be able to retire (i.e., to win the game), one must first *build up a retirement base* (funds, property, equity). Clearly, we must have enough resources accumulated to retire. Were this not the case, many more people would be retiring earlier. If it were too easy, though, some may never have worked at all!

There is the general belief among most people that after a certain number of years, one "deserves" to retire. The prospective retiree "did his share" and "made his contributions to life and society." Now, it is "someone else's turn," as the saying goes. Moreover, this person may be a little "tired" -- physically and mentally -- tired of the same routine, tired of the same lifestyle -- and, maybe, literally, just simply tired -- in need of some rest!

In any case, retirement generally connotes an *advanced seniority in age*. This would not be too bad, were it not for our existing feelings about old age. We have reviewed the notions we have acquired through the years about what's likely to happen to us when we reach these ripened plateaus. We also reviewed some common feelings about working and the advantages of working hard, succeeding, and being happy. Despite these ideas, we have accepted the possibility that we *can* leave work and still be happy.

For some of us, although we might otherwise be able to enjoy the fruits of retirement, it seems to be a real imposition that we must accept being old, too, before we can enjoy retirement. However, in our Retirement Game, it is apparent that you can't really have one without the other. They *do* go hand-in-hand. The Real World Game seems to be identical -- and that is where it really counts!

A Closer Look at the Seniors

Gee, I like that word -- "Seniors" -- it sounds so much

better than "old folks" -- or "the aging" or "the aged." Here is where that "opposite view" we anxiously were waiting for starts to appear. So, get ready for the "good news" part of our story.

A moment ago, we were sharing our observations of what we saw when we looked at a group of seniors. Then, to this we added the stories we had heard, and the lessons we had been taught. We concluded that, from a practical sense, it might be very difficult to believe that the "Golden Years" would be truly "golden."

We have noted that these unpleasant pictures, as real and dominant as they seem, are really not the only ones out there. Thankfully there are ample "other views" out there, too. For instance, how about those other retired seniors, who manage to continue on into advanced years with their good looks and good health? People in this group may exhibit some slightly eroded conditions, but their jolly good humor and optimistic outlook do not let us (or them) even think about any declining personal attributes. Their false teeth could fall right out on the floor and we'd probably miss it! We'd be so absorbed by their good company and so enthralled with their stories -- so happy just being around them -- that we would not notice anything bad, even the obvious.

These are happy people who exhibit happiness, and radiate love, joy, and inner peace. It is not unusual, either, that these particular seniors also are most interesting to be around. Some are downright entertaining. Their tenure and years have broadened and ripened their experiences. They are able to bring us innumerable, interesting, true-life accounts that attract and hold our attention, sometimes breathlessly.

For the moment, let's now, for identification purposes, label this second group of people, the "happy" ones, Type A. So that we won't get them mixed up with the former group --

the ones who seemed to be "headed down hill"-- let's call the other specimens, the unhappy, deteriorating ones, Type B.[8] Now, we have them -- Type A -- good, fun to be around, happy, interesting, and entertaining, maybe fewer in number, but definitely worth seeking out; and, Type B -- those whom we can more easily find and observe, those who are on the decline and who have stories and tales to match.

Our favorite group, of course, is Type A. We want to be in their company because they are fun to be with. Their happiness is infectious. Their stories and experiences are exciting and worthy of our attention -- or anyone's. Now, the good news is this: while our Type A specimens may be fewer in number, we *can* find them. We can find them -- *everywhere*!

We might wisely ask ourselves what makes Type A people so different? Why are they happy? Put more simply, why are some people happy and others not? These are fair questions and very germane to our study of finding happiness in retirement.

I believe Norman Vincent Peale comes to our rescue again.[9] He says that happy people are the people "who make it a habit to be happy." Dr. Peale also shares some additional insight when he says: "Who decides whether you shall be happy or unhappy? The answer -- you do!" Continuing, he quotes one of his favorites, Abe Lincoln, who once said: "People are about as happy as they make up their minds to be." Dr. Peale's wise counsel to each of us is to "make it a habit to be happy." We can all learn from these valuable words of advice.

We need to pry further into the lives of these happy people -- our Type A group. As we look deeper, we should see not only happy people in this group, but people who are truly *enjoying life*. That's what we all want too!

Why are our Type A people are truly enjoying life? What makes them so different from the rest? Well, if we were to carefully analyze and scrutinize the various attributes of our Type A people, we would undoubtedly find that there are many, many variables among them. However, our analysis should help us discover that each person in the Type A group exhibits a common attribute. These people have one thing in common: a *positive outlook on life*. Generally, they *harbor good thoughts*.

Again, Norman Vincent Peale comes to the rescue. He has a word of advice about thoughts and thinking in general. Dr. Peale counsels: "If happiness is determined by our thoughts, it is necessary to drive off the thoughts which make for depression and discontent."[10] After our studies on aging and retirement, doesn't this sound like especially sound advice for anyone approaching retirement?

The message certainly seems clear enough. We must somehow -- difficult as it might be -- learn to climb above any material observations or mental hurdles that are strewn in our pathway. Even in very difficult situations, like nursing homes, we must strive to keep our minds filled with healthy, joyful thoughts. The "magic" is this: As we get our thinking straight, we will, at that point, gradually find joy-filled days ahead. Then, it will be easier to close the door quickly on intruding, unhealthy thoughts -- thoughts which present mankind as aging and declining.

Please don't misinterpret this as being so blind (and Polyannaish) that we do not still see and hear calls of distress. We can always stand ready to help our neighbor in a moment of need. However, we should all learn and practice keeping a happy state of mind and disclaiming kinship to any condition which would rob us of happiness and propel us in the opposite, sad direction.

Being in control of our thinking probably sounds easy enough. In practice, though, I am sure we already know that this may be the biggest challenge of our lifetime. We could call this mighty conflict, "the battle with oneself." For myself, I try each day to learn more about how to watch and listen for good and happy thoughts. The battle is sometimes difficult, but the payoff is very great, indeed. It makes the mighty conquest worthwhile.

Since thoughts, (good or bad) come from people, doesn't it make good sense, also, to try to associate with good and happy people? These people who have good thoughts exude good, and dwell on happy stories. When we are with them, we find that their happiness is "catching." Does this mean that we should avoid (or shun) those whose lives and fortunes might not be so rosy? No, not necessarily. But, we don't have to dwell among them either and actually become a part of that environment -- letting some of their misery rub off on us. Often, we clearly have the choice.

The obvious exception is when we have a chance to change *their* views. This is sometimes possible, especially if they, themselves, want to change. Then, we really become the champion by winning them over to the right side. We might say we've moved a few Type B's over to the Type A side of the game board -- a real thrill!

Watching for the Type A's

Granted, then, that we want to find these "opposite views," but as much as possible, we really want to be around the Type A's. We know that they are out there. Why, then, is it so hard to make this a habit?

For a moment, let me share my own experience in observing large groups of older people, seniors. The best "laboratory" is perhaps our retirement facilities -- sometimes called retirement centers or extended care facilities. It brings large groups of older citizens together. I already referred to nursing homes several times. Sometimes this is simply part of a larger retirement center or retirement home -- a wing or section dedicated to taking care of larger groups of people with advanced health care needs. In other cases, a nursing home is a special place, that is totally dedicated to taking care of larger groups of people with advanced health problems. In any case, whether visiting a retirement center of a nursing facility, or joining a large group of seniors at a social meeting, there are some important lessons to be learned in being around any of these places, if we watch and observe the residents there.

My own dear mother spent more than nine years in the Army Distaff Hall. This is a Retirement Center for dependants of U.S. military personnel. It is located adjacent to beautiful and historic Rock Creek Park, in Washington, D.C.

When my mother first moved there, she was in reasonably good health, quite mobile, and pretty happy. She had a small, neat and orderly apartment on one of the upper floors. The nursing portion of the facility was on the basement floor. She spent about eight years in her apartment and then another one and a half years in the nursing section before passing on. Therefore, I was able to observe her and her friends in a variety of situations.

Initially, while my mother was in her apartment, she had maid service to help her keep her apartment straight, a nice evening meal, friends, entertainment, and transportation to all the nearby interesting places. She appeared to have nearly everything. She quickly became adjusted to her new surroundings, and made many friends.

Even with her apparent satisfaction, however, and not too long after she moved in, I observed that some of her friends and associates seemed to be consumed by discussing their aches and pains. They also seemed destined to talk about, "Who's sick now?" or "Has anybody heard what happened to Mrs. X who went to the hospital last week?" Without really meaning any harm, they just seemed destined to dwell on "bad news stories" -- reports of deterioration and near-tragedy. Sometimes I am sure it was just "idle talk," just making conversation. Many times, though, it seemed that they relished these stories of deterioration and were literally *projecting* their own lives into the pictures they were discussing. It was quickly apparent to me that these projections could very easily weave their way on into the consciousness of the listeners, unless they were extremely careful. Another thing: the participants in these sad stories and tales were likely, eventually, to take on a very gloomy (even morbid) viewpoint.

For example, about a year after my mother moved to the Distaff Hall, she told me somewhat jokingly one day, that the residents there called their retirement home: "The Finishing School." This was because, as my mother explained, "When you come here you are truly <u>finished</u>!" She laughingly concluded, "Most of the people here say we arrive in style by limousine and then depart in a pine box by hearse!" She remarked also that this was definitely a "favorite story" of the residents.

All that was intended to be humorous, and we both had a good laugh. However, their "favorite story" disclosed the way most of the residents really felt about the place and their lives out there. Underlying it all was a juncture and a destination (for each one of them) that was not too pleasant.

During the nine-plus year period, I visited my mother each week and sometimes several times during the week. I cannot say that she did not enjoy herself, her friends, or her life, especially at first. The continued discussions and negative talk and observations about the aging process, however, were slowly taking their toll.

I studied this process very closely during my many visits, observing very carefully my mother's condition and the conditions of several of her closest friends. I particularly watched for the resultant effects among her friends who were most vocal in "spreading the *bad news* stories." I also looked and searched hard for the exceptions -- the Type A people. Although the Type B's outnumbered the Type A's, the A's were there too! It was always good to see them, to talk to them, and to listen and be around them. They always made you feel good. Their stories offered such relief from the typical voices of gloom and doom. Our Type A's managed, somehow, to talk about the good news, generally trying to avoid opposite stories and discussions. It was obvious to me that the Type A's had their thinking straight and were harboring good thoughts.

Sometimes during my visits I would try to engage the Type B's in conversation, twisting around their sad tales, and offering some good news instead. I would take a negative remark and quickly turn it around into something pleasant. For example, if a resident said, "Oh, Mrs. X went to the hospital today. She was in such pain." I might retort, "Yes, but, you know she'll be back. She is a real fighter and has such inner strength and beauty." That would throw them off for a minute. I might continue with a "tale" of my own about someone I knew who had recovered from a similar ailment (or worse) and how they were now doing well. By taking an opportunity to twist each tale they spun into something with a pleasant ending, I found that some -- not all -- hungered for good news and welcomed it. I really believe such discussions helped bring them some relief as they glimpsed the brighter side of life.

Looking back now on my experiences, in some respects my visits there enabled me to see a live case study. Whether upstairs in the apartment area at the Distaff Hall or downstairs in the nursing facility, I found both Type B and Type A people -- ample numbers of each. I can report that, although our Type A's were friendly and cordial to all, they seemed to seek one another out and to cultivate their own type. They certainly felt more comfortable being around fellow optimists. I guess that the opposite is also the case. Even with our Type B's, there seems to be a certain camaraderie that builds with common attitudes and feelings. I wouldn't go so far as to say that these two types were in anyway separated, either consciously or unconsciously, but it came pretty close to that.

Let's dash back to the Type B's one final time. During my visits, I also began to understand why it was so easy to fall into the trap and become allied with the mainstream -- the B Group. It was, indeed, the *path of least resistance*. For one thing, there were more of them. The pull of the herd was a little more intense. Also, many were still harboring the "lessons of the past" -- the stories about aging and all the rest. Type B's simply could not become disassociated with those lessons.

Quite frankly, I could empathize with this, for no one would have trouble seeing the often sad and negative "pictures" being discussed and sometimes portrayed by the residents. They were quite prevalent, and one would have to be completely blind not to see them. I must admit that, in these circumstances, it must have required extraordinary efforts by any resident *not* to be consumed by the mass and their unhappy thoughts. Some, however, were able to meet this challenge. These were the heroic Type A's.

As I watched the residents, another interesting factor confirmed itself to me. Those who were overly aligned with the "evils of aging," those whose thoughts dwelt on these declining circumstances -- our Type B's -- seemed naturally to project these pictures on into their own lives in a very literal sense. For example, if Mrs. X fell, then "I" can expect to fall (and probably will). If Mrs. Y went to the hospital, then *so will "I."* Maybe it won't occur today or tomorrow, but it is coming. Sadly, and even somewhat mysteriously, these expectations generally came to pass.

Now, remember the good news. As noted, there were a few happy and joyful people at the Distaff Hall -- our Type A's. In visiting other, similar facilities, I have observed large numbers of Type A's everywhere. I have also seen them at all other places where seniors gather: old folk homes, retirement homes, hospitals, recreation centers, and at meetings of various senior associations and organizations (such as the AARP). The Type A's are out there. Our job is just to watch for them and find them. More than that, we want to be Type A too!

Putting Retirement to the Real Test

Earlier, we discussed Norman Vincent Peale's eleven components of happiness. What we want to do now is to take *each* one of Dr. Peale's components, and ask ourselves if retired life can meet the test with that component. If it can, then we should be able to conclude, comfortably, that one can retire and be happy too. That conclusion, along with our "right frame of mind" -- being determined to be a Type A -- will enable us to meet our first major requirement.

Let's begin by taking Dr. Peale's first component: **spiritual experience**. As we analyze this component, it should become clear that we ought to experience more (not less) spirituality in retirement than we did during our work life. We certainly should have more time available and probably more opportunity for our spiritual life. The changed pace should help too. All align on the side of retirement.

The next element, **deep inner peace**, may go hand-in-hand with finding spirituality. There should be no reason we cannot find inner peace anywhere -- retirement included. We can understand that we will have to *want it* and also might have to *work at it*, but if we want deep inner peace, we can have it. A lot will depend on how successful we are in finding important and satisfying things to do -- activities that can deliver inner peace and satisfaction. Again, we'll have more time available and that should help. We may even be able to go further and find more inner peace in retirement than we did at work. I have many friends who did.

Let's take the next two together: **serenity** and **joy**. Doesn't it seem reasonable that we should be able to find both of them in retirement? We certainly will enjoy more freedom of choice. Sure, a lot will depend on our approach and what we do with our retired life, but as we think about it together, it wouldn't make much sense to say that retirement rules them both out, would it?

The next two, **excitement** and **struggle**, seem to go together, too. These two may also seem to be at odds with joy and serenity, just discussed. Let's isolate them and see if retirement will meet the test. At first glance, a hyperactive work situation may seem better suited than retired life. It also may seem natural that there are more challenges and pressing demands at the workplace. Yet, couldn't we also label these "frustrations," in an unkind sense? In any case, on the surface the workplace may seem to better meet the test.

Suppose for a moment, though, that we have searched and found things in our retired life that we really like and want to do. Isn't it logical also to assume that some of these activities would provide a measure of genuine excitement and refreshment? For example, some probably will be new, fresh challenges, offering varying degrees of difficulty. Before in our work mode, we may have stayed clear of these types of activities, because, even though attractive, we didn't think we could find time to really enjoy them. Now, we could well find that the increased time on our hands enables us to acquire new talents or sharpen some of our old ones.

Going back to the question of whether or not we can find a few things that can provide the needed taste of excitement and even struggle, if we ponder for a few more moments, I believe we can think of several activities that clearly meet the test. If we can find these things, retirement will continue to meet the test. If you start squirming a little here, please bear with me. Shortly, I'll help you find just the right activities in retirement, along with the right combinations, to keep your interest, your excitement -- and maybe even your desire to struggle a little (if you really want it) -- all at a high level. We'll get into that in a little while.

Our intensive studies will enable us to examine and study **health** and **finances** at some length, also. For now, let's say that there are no reasonable grounds for concluding that retired life cannot meet the health and finances test as well. We will even throw in **good digestion**, since our coverage of the health aspects is very comprehensive. I believe we'll see how retirement should, in fact, offer us increased opportunities.

This leaves **loving someone** and **having someone to love us**. We easily recognize these two components as two of the main elements of happiness, true happiness. Whether we are at work or retired, the elements of loving should be constant. We may, again, because of having more time, enjoy even *increased* opportunities to cultivate true love in our lives. Think about a man and wife who, before retirement, had trouble finding much time together. Now, they have a total lifetime to share. They also have each other to share it with. Shouldn't they both find *more* love? It certainly seems so.

I hope we can all agree, then, with our brief analysis of the eleven components of happiness, that retirement should have no difficulty in meeting the test. Retired life should be able to provide *at least* as much opportunity for happiness as one would find when working. In fact, with the extra time and maturity gained, maybe we can do *even better* -- go farther.

Let's accept it. You don't have to be working to be happy! Retirement meets the test. It *can* deliver happiness.

Accept It: We CAN Find Real Happiness in Retirement!

Now the brightest of all prospects yet: When we acknowledge the fact that finding happiness in retirement (and old age) *is* possible, we are ready to move to the next plateau. We are prepared to entertain the thought that we may be happier in our new retired life than we've ever been before. In the analysis of Dr. Peale's eleven components of happiness, we occasionally added that in retirement, we may be able to do better or go farther. Now, let's think of it together. Not only is the premise that man must work to be happy a myth, but retirement bringing happiness -- *even at a higher level* -- can be our newly found heritage.

What we've really been doing is getting our thinking straight. We've been discovering (or maybe rediscovering, for some) various ways we can look at people and ourselves. We have our happy, positive state of mind, and we want all want to be Type A's. We could say, at this point, we have about cleaned out all the cobwebs! We can also clearly see that a person can mature, retire, and find real happiness.

The process is like building a house. First, we lay the foundation and then we bring the house on up to the sky, piece by piece. In this analysis, we have laid the first block of our solid foundation. Now, let's get on to finding out how to lay additional, solid building blocks to our already well-started, positive foundation. Then, we can explore other secrets of building our happy retirement house.

3

LAYING THE FOUNDATION FOR REAL HAPPINESS

IT IS HOPED that we can now agree that seniors, older people, can be happy and that it is possible to find happiness in retirement. Further, we are determined to find it! We could at this point lay out the recipe, the detailed how-to-do-its. Yet even with our positive attitude of knowing that a happy retirement awaits us, we could still find rough sledding without three other foundation blocks. Having any one of the three, or better yet -- the entire package -- will make our quest for retirement happiness easier and more certain.

Getting Ready Financially

First, we must be sure that we have laid a solid financial foundation for retirement. Most people will agree that money does not buy happiness, as the old saying goes. However, it is absolutely basic that you have to have a solid financial program and sufficient funds before you can entertain retiring. It becomes, therefore, a given that one's financial status provides some important parameters in retirement planning. Whatever retirement plan we develop, it must be consistent with our own financial base. Otherwise, our retirement life could be seriously restricted. Even worse, all the money laid up for retirement could be spent someday, and we would either be destitute or forced back into a work regimen. Either could be catastrophic.

While all of this may seem quite basic, the sad, hard facts remain that many people do not give enough thought to their post-retirement finances. They also do not start early enough. Some even get a little frightened as they start giving the problem serious thought. We have all heard stories about how inflation keeps cost of living expenses going up while retirement income seems to be fairly well frozen and static. Without good projection of our finances, then, the future could look somewhat dangerous and uncertain.

Although the detailed treatment of financial planning for retirement is beyond the scope of this book, I do have a few key suggestions. (As you work your own financial plan, you might use these points as a checklist to see that you have covered everything on this important topic.)

First, any financial plan should include a very detailed examination of your post retirement income and expenses. Be sure to include all projected costs and assets. Also, add in a reasonable amount for contingencies -- the unknown circumstances that could impact your overall financial status. It is a good idea to write down your own estimates in an orderly fashion. For both income and expenses, this written list can be analyzed, reviewed and rewritten to assure that you are including the major categories and are making reasonable estimates in all cases.

Go over your own monthly and annual expenses to be

sure you have not forgotten anything. Big items like mortgage payments, car expenses, utilities, food and clothing, entertainment and travel are likely to be quickly included. But don't forget some of the smaller expenses, such as dental care, that could throw you way off.

For income, the same applies. Put everything down in writing and make every effort to include everything. Retirement annuities, social security, and large items will be recalled quickly. It is easy, though, to forget to list dividends on that stock which pays so infrequently, or on each investment income. Your last income tax statement may jog your memory.

Each item on the list, both income and expenses, should be carefully challenged and thought through. Be sure you make *reasonable estimates* based on past records. Take the "Devil's Advocate" position. Be tough. It will pay off.

When you are satisfied with your worksheets, the next step should be to assure that you have enough excess income, over expenses, to retire. By this I mean enough surplus finances to meet your standard of retired living. How much should that be? Many experts who have studied this situation report that a person will need about 70 percent of pre-retirement income for a comfortable retirement. For instance, one says: "...you generally can expect to live as well in retirement as you do now on 70% to 80% of your current income."[11] Another reports: "If you want to live in retirement the way you do now, you'll need only about two thirds to three quarters of the income you have now. Why? Because a lot of your current expenses are business related: transportation, clothes, business luncheons, gifts, entertainment. You'll also have increased tax advantages in retirement."[12] A few others even give us a range-somewhere between 60 and 70 percent. I'd be a little concerned, though, if you drop below the 60 percent level.

I frankly had not heard about these retirement income parameters when I retired. However, in checking, I was pleasantly surprised to see that our own retirement income was about 72.6% of our pre-retirement income. We just made it across the 70% mark! With our current income, I might add, my wife and I have not given up a single thing that we used to enjoy. Also, we still save a little money each year. So I believe the 70% rule is a very good guide to follow.

Finally, if you have any doubts about the soundness of your retirement financial base, it might be well to do a little in-depth research. Most of our public libraries are loaded with good and reliable information about retirement planning. This includes a lot of helpful financial advice. For example, you might find Edward L. Palder's book, *The Retirement Sourcebook*, very useful.[13] If you still have doubts, you should consider contacting an expert financial planner. These planners are widely available and are not too expensive. If you plan to call on outsiders, however, take some time in making your selection. You have a lot at stake here, and you want the best possible advice.

Let's assume, then, with good financial planning, our retired specimens (you and I) have laid up sufficient funds to retire and have a solid financial plan. Somewhere along the way our financial plan should be able to tell us how much is left over at the end of any given period. This "left over" becomes our "play money." Does it look sufficient? Not to worry. We should (in most cases) be able to work it out, whether the *play money pile* is large or small. But, our planned activities might be slightly (or even drastically) curtailed or modified when we consider "real world" financial constraints.

For instance, for a lot of us, there probably will not be many "world voyage trips" available annually (or even in a five-year period). They are very expensive -- starting at around $10,000 or $15,000 per couple, depending on where you want to go and how you want to travel. Also, enjoyable as these world voyages may be, we might find other things that would be equally satisfying.

What about money for a hideaway, that "second home" -- you know, a home in the mountains or at the beach. Many of us think about this pretty seriously as we approach retirement. A second home in Florida at West Palm Beach, in California at Palm Springs, in the Ski Resort Area of Vail, Colorado, on the Big Island of Hawaii, or at some other exotic location, could present even more severe financial demands for many of us. With good planning, however, something a little less lavish and in closer proximity might be in the cards. If we find that we just can't manage a second home, there should be little concern; there are still many other things out there that will be satisfying and rewarding.

The important point, here, is to carefully consider how much play money we really have. The size of our pile will drive our choices of the activities that we will shortly develop and incorporate into firm daily and weekly routines. Again, don't worry. With good planning, we should be able to work it out. As I have said before, if we had all the money in the world, we'd probably find that money does not buy happiness. For now, though, let us just know that, together, we'll explore how to carve out a retirement routine that is very satisfying. You will see that it will not be totally dependent on financial resources. We will design the plan so that there will be several choices, within a wide range of finances.

Let's leave this first foundation block, then, with the hope that we have enough money to retire. Also, let's hope that we will be able to recognize any financial limitations that might influence our choices in developing firm retirement programs and schedules.

Getting Healthy and Staying Healthy

The second foundation block is learning how to seek (and find) good health. Put bluntly, *we must get healthy and stay healthy.*

All of us know people who lost their health and, from their sickbeds, acclaimed that health is the most precious commodity. We probably also have friends who declare, "With good health you have everything. Without it, you have nothing." There is a lot of truth in that. Certainly, we could have all the tricks in the book for becoming happy, but if our health is lacking, it would be difficult to reach the pinnacle of total happiness. Let's consider for a moment how to become healthy and, then, how to stay that way.

Getting healthy, of course, depends on the person and the case at hand. For those who take care of their bodies -- watch their diet, exercise regularly, get plenty of rest, maintain a good mental attitude and everything else that is commonly considered essential to health -- the task of attaining good health should be easy. Those in this group may almost be there now. We'll return to you in a moment.

Let's look at the opposite end of the spectrum. What about those of us who may not presently be at the peak of health? Let's include even those who may be bordering on some kind of illness. Here we have our work cut out. The task remains to become as healthy as we can -- to give ourselves a shot at a good starting point.

A Person Who Has Health Needs

Let's take this last case first and work our way back to our model of a healthy person as an objective starting point.

How does one rapidly reach an optimum health level? Naturally, that depends on the person and the individual needs and problems involved. We can be happy, though, that there are some things that each "prescription" would have in common. Let's take a few examples.

First, say a person is recovering from a very serious malady, like a heart or circulatory problem. The physician prescribes a lot of rest; mild, supervised exercise; a very careful diet; and continued, close monitoring. Should we change that? Absolutely not! However, with rest, exercise, and a properly tailored diet, the human body, itself, has the natural ability to do marvelous things to recuperate.

Let's pause for a moment and consider some of the observations and findings of Dr. Hans Selye of Montreal. You may be acquainted with the works of this famous physician.[14] Dr. Selye is known all over the world for his studies of stress, its impact on the human body, and the fundamentals of aging. His research and studies go back to 1936. Dr. Selye argues persuasively that the body, along with all of its marvelous components, is well designed to stay healthy by employing the forces of nature. He also shares his studies on how the human body employs its own built-in defense mechanisms to cure itself and to stay young. Dr. Selye endeavors to prove that the body is equipped to cope with the stress and other conditions which bring about "old age." However, perhaps of more interest in our pursuits, Dr. Sclye also argues that the body can heal itself. This notable doctor proclaims that the body's strong defenses may be the only real "cure" there is. He explains that medicine, and even surgery, often succeeds by simply augmenting and reinforcing the body's own natural defenses. Hey, this is pretty heavy stuff here! Whether you and I are ready to accept these arguments in their full context, is not the point. It is important, however, to recognize in some measure that the body does have strong *natural* healing abilities and that these inherent capabilities have a powerful impact on our lives. Think for a moment about some of the cases we've observed in our own experiences and the resultant favorable outcomes.

Watching Our Diet-Controlling Our Weight

Remember that we were dealing with a person who was a little behind at the start. He or she needed to catch up in order to start at an optimum level of health. What should that person do? Where should he or she start? Well, whether prescribed or not, it makes good sense, regardless of the malady, that people in this recovery group should carefully watch their diet. I am sure this includes watching daily calorie and fat intake. Some might be well advised to measure and record both of these in crucial cases.

It seems obvious that we should all attain and maintain a weight as close to the ideal as possible. It is widely recognized that most of our countrymen are overweight. If you happen to be in this category, you've got a lot of company. For example, recent national surveys report that about three out of four men are overweight. Women were only slightly better off. This should be a major, national concern.

Underlying the importance of weight control is its relation to heart disease. One reliable source reports: "Studies have shown those middle-age men who are 30 percent or more over their normal weight have twice the risk of a heart attack compared to other middle-age men of normal weight."[15] So, especially for older people (excuse me -- seniors), weight control is even more vital. For some of us, attaining our "right weight" could take some time. Still, none of us should be satisfied until our weight is in the "good range" for our age, sex and build. We should also make a commitment to do whatever it takes to keep our weight at this acceptable level. This sounds easy enough, but this is where the going really gets tough -- keeping our weight at a fairly constant level.

Some experts advise us to take a "diet vacation," eating whatever we like for a short period. Some people go on this diet vacation on an occasional weekend and then are *very* careful the following week. Several weight counselors believe this program is one of the best ways to keep weight off, long-term. You might want to try it.

Hey now, don't throw the book down and say, "I quit -- I've already tried dieting and, for me, it didn't work!" Even if you never reach your ideal weight range and are far outside the mark, I'd seriously counsel you to keep the old bathroom scale handy, work at it, and stay with it. Keep track of your progress and don't be satisfied with less than continuous improvement. Haven't we all seen many, many people who have overcome weight problems? For instance, how about Oprah Winfrey? She lost more than 87 pounds and even ran the marathon. It looks as though she will be able to keep her weight down. The good news is that all of us can do it, too -- if we really want to!

For myself, I've always had a tendency to be slightly on the plump side. The same goes for my wife, Helen, although to a lesser degree. We have both found, too, that things don't seem to get any better with age. Yet, in our own case, our friends who know us well often tell us how good we look -- and I'm sure they are talking about our physical bodies, too. I am 5'10" and weigh 170 pounds. Helen is 5'1" and weighs 117. I'd say, for now, we both are pretty close to being "just right."[16] We both weigh in right after our morning exercise workouts (discussed below) to keep close track of our weight status. In addition, Helen very carefully watches our fat intake in our daily meals -- whether we are eating in or out. While we don't keep a written track of our daily intake, we both monitor our fat and calorie consumption at each meal. I believe if one does this carefully, it may be possible to avoid detailed, written records. Again, it is all based on the needs of the individual.

An Active Exercise Program

Next, regardless of our weight, we need to develop an active exercise program. For best results, older people require some exercise each day. As we get older, we may find that we tire more easily and just don't feel like exercising. (I've heard that one a hundred times.) We have to be very careful here. Such an attitude may lead to inactivity -- a real killer.

Before we get into the nuts and bolts of exercise, it would be well to flag a couple of cautions. First, medical professionals all agree that an older person who wants to start an exercise program should first consult a physician. Second, our experts also advise any exercise beginner to slowly and steadily work up to peak achievement. This is good advice regardless of the exercises in a given program. Start with a relatively short distance, fewer repetitions, and a smaller number of movements -- for a short period of time, initially. Gradually, the body can tolerate, and in fact enjoys, extended physical stress for longer periods of time, as the optimum is approached. Such a gentle start has the bonus of making any new program more agreeable to both mind and body. The obvious consequence is our ability to stick with the program. This is an important objective.

Let's now consider what kind of exercise we need. I've found in my own life (and observed in countless others) that, as a minimum, successful programs must engage the large muscle groups and be rhythmical and aerobic. The heart rate and oxygen intake must be stretched. This can be attained by something as simple as walking two or three miles daily at a brisk pace. Some health experts say this is the very best and safest exercise for older folks. They praise the marvels of "just plain walking." One authority says: "Brisk walking (3 ½ to 5 mph) may burn as much as 81 percent of the calories burned in running, and fast walking (5 mph or more) actually burns 100 calories more than jogging because you exert more energy taking strides in walking than you do running."[17]

Your exercise program may center on jogging -- careful, listen to the knees, hips, and ankle joints; running -- for the real "jocks" -- again, watch the impact; jazzercise or aerobic dancing -- with a group, tape or TV program; bench stepping -- careful of the impact; or the use of all kinds of home gym equipment -- favorites are treadmills, stair steppers, ski machines, easy riders and stationary bicycles. To round out the list we could add a few others: swimming, skating, road biking and just plain dancing.

With any exercise program, it is first very important to include some good before and after stretching. Also it is essential to get the heart-rate up and kept at a higher level for several minutes. A good guide for duration, according to the experts, is a minimum of 20 to 30 minutes.

Then, the next question is: *how often* do we need to exercise? You may have observed that experts generally agree that "every other day," for at least 20-30 minutes is sufficient.[18] For me and my wife Helen, we find that we need to do "our thing" nearly every day. We try to do this, perhaps excluding Sundays, with sometimes another pause at midweek. We really try to listen to our bodies. Most weeks, though, we hit it almost every day. As with a lot of things, I believe our bodies will be our best counsel to address the question of frequency and, maybe, duration as well.

Finally, if we really want to get serious and "scientific" to boot, we might want to take a closer look occasionally at our aerobic performance. Experts tell us to attain an optimum heart rate for about 30 minutes during the aerobic exercise period. We determine this "optimum 'heart rate by subtracting our age from 220 and multiplying this number by 70 percent (60 percent for older people or those just starting an active exercise program). For example, then, for a 70-year-old, this "optimum" heart rate would be $(220 - 70) \times 0.6 = 90$ beats per minute. To calculate your pulse (heartbeats), an easy way is to count the number of beats for 10 seconds and then multiply by six. (Personally, I rarely monitor my own heart rate this carefully, and I am not sure that most people need to watch it that closely. However, if you want to do it, you know how.)

Weight Training

In addition to aerobics, I am a firm believer in weight training. I believe we really need to add some kind of weight training to our exercise program. By this I mean giving the muscles and bones some convenient form of resistance. I've personally never found that isometrics, i.e., having one muscle group pull against another, a la Charles Atlas, did the trick. Weights, however, seem to me to meet the need, practically and conveniently.

Let me share with you why I am so sold on weights. (If weights don't sound particularly appealing, don't tune me out yet; in a minute I'll show you how easy it is to use them.) If we closely observe the *engineering* of our bodies, we'll see the intricate way our bones are tied to our muscles, via tendons and ligaments. They are all marvelously integrated into a unified system, but one really depends on the other. Thus when we strengthen a given muscle, we strengthen the adjoining ligament and tendon. You strengthen one and you strengthen all in a given *system*. This increased strength greatly benefits the total bone mass, which in older people, we are told, is in a constantly regressive state. In other words, the bones need all the help they can get. That's just where stronger muscles (with adjoining ligaments and tendons) come to our relief; they help the bones be all that they can be.

With our stronger muscles and bones, common bodily tasks become more pleasant. Things like moving, walking, sitting, standing -- or even running, for that matter -- are just simply easier.

Let me show you how easily weights can be used. As a young man, I experimented with barbells and weights as many young people do, but I was never attracted for long periods. It seemed too much like hard work! I concluded, in those days, that I just did not like weights particularly. Then about four years ago, I bought a set of small, hand-held, eight-pound dumbbells. I found that these little dumbbells are terrific. They are padded and easy to handle. They came with a small booklet which suggests some exercises while standing, sitting, bending and lying on the floor. I was surprised to see how much exercise I could plow into the pectorals, the biceps and triceps, the abdominals, and the back muscle groups with these relatively small weights. It was a matter of doing any particular exercise right and doing many repetitions, but I seemed to get a lot out of them. In a very short period, my arms, stomach and back seemed to be better toned, tighter and stronger.

Then about three years ago, my son, who is into Nautilus Weight Program training at the local gyms -- and looks like a million dollars, incidentally -- suggested that I supplement the small dumbbells with a barbell and relatively light weights. He also suggested I get a small exercise bench with leg lift and arm, butterfly attachments. Well, I found a small, 110-pound barbell set and an ideal weight bench. (The bench, made by Weider, is available at almost any discount or sporting goods store.) Like the dumbbells, both of the new acquisitions came with short exercise program booklets. In a matter of a few days, I had supplemented my daily, longstanding 2½ mile jog with weights. Now my regular program routine calls for weights (about 30-40 minutes per session) -- using both the dumbbells and the barbells -- about three times each week. On alternate days I rotate my weight training days with vigorous aerobic exercise. For me, this is either a two-mile jog, a four-mile fast walk, or -- in bad weather -- 30 minutes on my Health Rider®. (I also frequently use the Health Rider® when I want variety or a break from my regular routine.)

While we are talking about exercise equipment, let me share with you some other personal experiences. These may save you a little time and effort, and maybe money too. I used to have a rowing machine and a stationary bike. Both were of good quality, but neither did much for me and were pretty boring, to boot. The rowing machine is supposed to help strengthen the back. Using mine, however, seemed to only tire the back and sometimes even resulted in minor (but prolonged) soreness. The stationary bike gave me a very good aerobic workout, but occasionally it also seemed to bother my knees and back slightly. In addition it took first place on the "most boring" list.

I then looked closely at several other pieces of home exercise equipment. These included stair steppers, treadmills and my Health Rider®. First I bought a highly recommended stair stepper. Like the bicycle, it gave me a good aerobic workout. However, it gradually picked a fight with my knees on many of the days that I used it. So, the stair stepper was abruptly abandoned.

I never got around to treadmills, although I have used them in gyms and hotels when traveling. I have found that they offer good aerobic conditioning, but I am not sure about what they could do to the knees and hips in the long haul. There seems to be quite a bit of impact. In prolonged use, they might take their toll. Still, for me, "the jury is out" on treadmills.

Now let me tell you about my more recent acquisition, our Health Rider®. This is a U.S. manufactured, high quality piece of equipment. It is what's called a "Total Body Workout" machine. It concentrates on the large muscle groups and is perfect for aerobic exercise. Burning a lot of calories and delivering a good workout to the heavy muscle groups, it also helps the extra pounds stay off. As a bonus, the machine adds to aerobics and fat burning, deep muscle stretching, and even muscle building. It is absolutely noiseless and has zero impact anywhere. This is especially welcomed by the old hip, knee and ankle bones. At this point we have had the new machine for nearly three years and continue to praise its virtues. If I sound excited and thrilled about the machine, I am. So is my wife. She now supplements her regular low impact TV dance program with the Health Rider®. She does this at least three times a week, to assure that she gets her aerobic workout.

For those other machines which I discussed (and for others I did not), they still may be O.K. for some people. I'm thinking of ski machines, stepping stools, and others. I know lots of people who use and like them all. My only "P.S." for any of this equipment is to watch the impact. Particularly be careful about the knees, hips, and ankles. Old bones need to be protected; they just don't need too much impact. That is one reason I am starting to cut back on my jogging and substituting the Health Rider® more frequently. When I want some fresh air exercise, I get out and just simply walk (fast). As a final word, please be careful about machines. Some can be so boring and cause such strain on the body that you can get turned off quickly. This presents great dangers. We don't want anything to take us away from our exercising, since it is so vital to our health.

Exercise Program for Women

On the distaff side, let me share some of the things my wife Helen has done and is doing to stay fit. (As I mentioned, she is presently involved in a low impact exercise program.) Helen has always been active and, for more than 20 years, has participated in various ladies exercise programs. A few years ago she designed and developed a short 30-minute program for her friends. Her program consisted of various stretching and muscle tensioning exercises, along with a short jog in place at the conclusion. All of this was carried out to the rhythm of taped, modern music. Her program became so popular that she presented daily exercise classes for the local church for more than a year. Moreover, when we were frequent travelers in my prior employment, program planners always persuaded her to conduct her 30-minute ladies' exercise classes during our meetings and conventions. They usually offered her a choice spot on the program. The 50-200 wives who traveled with their husbands to our conventions praised these sessions.

When our travels tapered off, Helen sought other exercise outlets. She tried gyms and liked them; however, they were not convenient. Then about five years ago, Helen became vigorously engaged in a TV program called *Body Electric,* with Margaret Richard. This is a Public Broadcasting Station program beamed in from Florida. Helen uses the program for 30 minutes daily. The good thing about that particular program is that it has aerobic exercises, stretches and light weight training. They use 2-4 pound ladies' dumbbells on most of their workouts. Helen is really sold on the program. When she needs some outside fresh air or a good boost to her aerobic training, she augments her TV programs with either long walks (going with me) or exercising on the Health Rider®. Her program must be working, because she is, indeed, the perfect picture of good health.

Getting Plenty of Rest

Now let's get back to our first case -- remember, the not-too-healthy person who needs to improve his or her health status at the outset. I firmly believe that following good diet and exercise programs, supplemented by *getting plenty of rest,* should do the trick. When I say rest, I mean at least seven (preferably eight) hours of sleep each night. For some, taking a 30- to 45-minute rest in the afternoon also helps. Again, our best advisors should be our own bodies. The main thing is to get plenty of rest and avoid getting overtired.

My wife and I have been fortunate in never having a sleeping problem. I could count on one hand the times either of us has had difficulty going to sleep or staying asleep. I attribute a lot of that to getting a good workout during the day. We also make a conscious effort during our waking hours to avoid sitting or being immobilized for too long a period. Therefore when night comes and we retire, we usually fall asleep at once.

I realize that not all people are so fortunate. I cannot imagine too many things worse than not being able to sleep or get your rest. I do know, however, that a lot has been written about the subject. Most sleep experts seem to agree that avoiding drugs helps the sleep process. Many even counsel against the mildest forms of sleeping pills. I believe that is very sound advice. Anything that tinkers with the mind too much seems to be approaching the edge and could be fraught with hidden dangers. Most experts advise drinking milk at bedtime. Milk seems to be a natural sedative, inducing sleep. Some add supplementing with a *very small* nighttime snack -- a cookie or graham cracker (careful -- not too much -- just a bite or two with the milk). Experts also suggest doing no exercise just prior to bedtime, having short periods of peace and quiet (reading or watching TV) just before going to bed, retiring only when we're sleepy, drinking no alcohol, and trying to have pleasant thoughts. These really sound like good common sense suggestions and sound advice for us all.[19]

What About the Person Who is Healthy Already?

Let's now move back to where we started, to the person who is already at the peak of health. You may feel very comfortable with our healthy specimen. You may, as I do, better identify with this type of person.

I honestly do not believe there was a single day in my nearly 45 years of employment when I could not go to work because of illness. I've always been healthy. In the Army, except on two occasions, I "maxed" the annual P.T. test with a perfect 300 score. I played football, basketball and tennis in high school. In college I engaged in all kinds of intramural sports. I've always exercised, because I like it. I especially like the great, soaring feeling of well-being that a good workout brings. So if you are more at home with the healthy individual in our example, you are keeping company with me.

When we talk about our healthy specimen -- the person who has everything, health-wise -- we mean the person who has about the right weight, maintains a good diet, has no rest problems, and engages in a good exercise program regularly. Regardless of where we are today, that healthy specimen is the person we all want to be (and where we want to stay). What should such a person do or change? The answer is quite obvious: not very much. Once we've reached our health pinnacle, our job is to maintain that level. How do we do that?

In discussing our earlier specimen the one who started out with some health problems -- we outlined various programs to help that person get on track and stay on track. This included diet and weight control, an active exercise program, and getting plenty of rest. Assuming our fit specimen -- on the opposite, pleasant side of the tracks -- is doing all of this about right, he or she just wants to develop the discipline and resolve to "keep it up." That should result in a continued, healthy state. If, perchance, something starts to *sag,* then that element can be emphasized and *shored up.* For example, if for some reason you start having sleeping problems, you can work on that. If your weight slowly starts to creep upward, you can isolate that as the key problem and work that out. The advice offered initially to our first specimen -- the one lacking good health -- should be helpful in guiding us back to where we want to be.

Now in between the two extremes, the healthy and not-too-healthy specimens, we have still another group. These are the people who are not in desperate health circumstances but certainly are not yet at the peak of performance. What about them? Well, again looking at what we just prescribed for those in our first needy group, the suggested programs should still apply. Of course the regimens will have to be tailored appropriately. Add a little here, take a little there, and apply the same general principles. Eventually, though, we all want to reach our peak health level and stay there, That's our objective.

The Importance of Observation in Our Daily Lives

Before we leave this important building block -- getting healthy and staying that way -- let's discuss one final proposition. You know, you really don't have to be a full-fledged expert in the medical field to have some pretty solid information on the way you feel and the way your body responds. Our bodies speak to us all the time. That is why, when you have a problem and you go to see a doctor, he asks you very pointedly: "What's wrong?" "How do you feel?" "Where does it hurt?" Notice, too, that he listens very carefully to what you say. This may be the most important part of his diagnosis -- what you are telling him -- or, more precisely, what you are relaying to him from what your "own body" is telling you. His expert diagnosis proceeds from there.

Every human being has this built-in communicator -- the human body. We reside within human bodies. This body is speaking to us almost constantly. In addition, we see other people, many other people, in different circumstances throughout the day. We have a real opportunity to observe and to listen to what their human bodies are saying to them, too. As we grow older, the number of such experiences multiplies, both from our own body experiences and from those of others. Therefore, it should not seem so strange that we, ourselves, are privy to some very expert opinions. True, maybe most of us have not been to medical school, but we know something (quite a lot, in fact) about living with (and inside) the old human body. Our own observations count; they count very much, and they should not be taken lightly.

Upon close examination, we discover that science is really a set of applied rules and principles based on observed trials and errors. No one particular science is *totally* perfect, including the field of medical science and engineering. How many doctors and nurses have we seen who will frankly admit that medical science, as advanced and excellent as it is, is still left with many questions when it comes to human health. One day we read that we should not eat butter, rather margarine; within a month the health experts say butter is O.K. and that margarine is suspect. So, that's the way life is on this planet.

It is a continuing set of unfurling circumstances with real world, human actors (us). The neat trick is to find the time and energy amid our fleeting events of living to observe, watch, catalogue and make tentative postulates, eventually leading to not-so-tentative decisions.

This especially applies to human health. The human animal is a perfect laboratory. It is perfect because we ourselves (the observers -- the scientists in the lab) are within the human body ourselves. That gives us a chance, constantly, to check out the validity and reliability of our observations. While this presents some dangers of "in-house bias," I don't believe we should be overly concerned about that, especially if we are reaching sound decisions. (We'll know!) The real point here is that we all have our very own private set of observations in this crucible of life, so that we can *know*, generally, what makes sense and what does not. This is very important in dealing with health in our own human bodies. The doctor may make the final diagnosis and prescribe the cure, but when we listen to our own bodies, we get valuable signals -- in fact, valuable *first* signals.

We have another advantage: advancing age helps us with these experiments. Our increased age multiplies our experience by giving us more observations. It follows, then, that our decisions should be better and sounder as we grow older.

When the need arises, we can always ask ourselves: "Does this make sense?" "Are we really doing what's best for us?" "Is there a better way to do it?" We should not demean our feelings, this "silent voice" that is speaking to us. It can often set us on the right track and keep us there. Again, this seems to doubly apply to health issues, especially if our own human body is concerned.

Let's now turn to the final foundation block.

Getting Close to God

While our finances and health are extremely important in getting ready for a happy retirement, this last ingredient may be the key to the whole thing. I realize that anyone who addresses this topic in an open forum must watch how the subject is presented, so I will try to exercise the utmost care in saying what I believe needs to be said. Please know that I certainly understand that what I have found in my own life will not necessarily apply to everybody. In the interest of trying to be most candid and helpful, though, permit me to relay some pertinent experiences which may have some bonus value to nearly everyone.

The aging process frequently brings more challenges with the passing of time: physical, mental and, sometimes, financial. I won't say this is natural, but the human, living process tries to make this all seem very real. In my own life, though, I personally find that whatever the challenge, however serious the consequences, I always have a friend out there to help me. For me, that friend is God.

I find that God truly answers prayer. He always meets my daily needs. For this friend, I find that no concern is too big and no question is too small. During my own trials and moments of pain and difficulty, I've proven it over and over again, with a long series of successes. With every single success, or trial, my faith gets stronger. I also believe that this special, ever present, all powerful, all knowing, ever loving friend -- God -- is there for *each one of us,* if we want it. I suspect it matters little which church, forum or congregation we align with, but I flatly affirm that in this life one needs some outside, special help. This applies especially to older people, with the apparent momentous set of threats and voids that might appear.

In my own life, I find that there is a deep, quieting, soothing effect from acknowledging and *feeling* the presence of God. Something deep inside says: "All is well. You are safe and secure. You are under the shadow of His mighty wing."[20]

To illustrate the comfort of keeping God close, let me return for a brief moment to my experiences in visiting my mother at the Army Distaff Hall. During the final months of my mother's stay at Distaff Hall, when she was in the nursing center, she and her roommate became very despondent with the passing of time. (I'm sure nobody knows how dismal and monotonous such an existence can be until they've actually lived that experience.) Anyway, when I visited with them, I always tried to cheer them up, finding something funny or light to talk about. That helped, but one Saturday morning, I happened to have my Bible in the car and I asked them (my mother and her roommate) if they would like for me to read the Bible to them. My mother's friend, especially, welcomed this; her eyesight had dimmed so that she had trouble reading anything, and she really liked the Scriptures. So I brought in the Bible and read -- mostly from Psalms.

After a few moments of reading, I noticed an atmosphere of love, peace and harmony that started to prevail. Both my mother and her friend had expressions of joy and peace in their eyes and on their faces as they smilingly approved of what they heard. When I departed that day, I noted that their peacefulness continued. What satisfaction this brought to all!

With the success of this first undertaking, I continued the Bible readings about once a week -- usually on Saturday. (That was the day that most residents in the nursing wing had the greatest number of visitors.) Hardly noticing it, I observed that as I started the readings inside my mom's room, several other ladies from adjacent rooms would pull up chairs -- in the room, or even out in the hallway. In a couple of weeks, the audience expanded to about 10-15 each time I read. The real bonus was that for every single one of those who listened, there seemed to be a residual peacefulness that lasted, sometimes even throughout the week. This was reported to me by the nurses and attendants at Distaff Hall.

Let's close this topic on this high note. It would be totally inappropriate for me (or anyone except maybe a member of the clergy) to lay out an unsolicited recipe for getting to know and work with God. This gets very personal and somewhat ecclesiastical, However, I must avow that, regardless of one's earthly status, there will come a time when things go easier with divine direction and assistance. This pertains, as well, to retirement and the entire aging process. Enough said.

4

THE PROCESS

L ET'S review. We first looked at retired people and found that many were not happy. Then we said that before we could build our house -- the figurative house being the recipe for finding happiness in retirement -- we first needed to lay a firm foundation. Further, we agreed, perhaps tentatively, to accept that [1] **anyone can find happiness in retirement** and that we were determined to find it. This was our first foundation block. To this cornerstone, we added three other foundation blocks: [2] **getting ready financially,** [3] **getting healthy** and staying that way, and finally, [4] **making friends with God** and trusting Him.

With our solid foundation in place, we should now be ready to build the house on up to the sky. We will first closely look at *a process* that involves taking a very careful inventory of what we will call "appealing things" to do. We'll actually make ourselves a list. We'll take plenty of time to develop this list, subjecting it to all kinds of analyses and tests. The list will be the very heart and soul of our retirement planning, and we want to do it right.

So that we won't forget anything, we'll make plenty of room for things that happen just once in a while, maybe once a year. We'll even learn how to make early adjustments to accommodate changing times, to assure that we have variety, and to guarantee that we never, ever experience boredom. That is fatal anytime, but it is especially so in retirement.

After we have developed our firm list of "appealing things" to do, we will map out our retirement days, weeks and months. We will try to work in our favorite things, loading our schedules to assure that we stay busy. In fact, if we do our job right, we'll be very busy all the time -- but remember, we'll *only* be doing the things we like and want to do. As we weave in our favorite things, we will also learn to group our activities so that we keep our days varied. This will prompt us, daily, to eagerly look forward to getting up and living our fun days of retirement. While we are doing all of this, we will review several examples and entertain a lot of suggestions. When we are finished, we will have our very own, specially tailored and unique retirement plan.

We will deliberately avoid getting too formal or structured in our concept or approach. As we think about our own fledgling plan unfolding, however, it would help if we had some pretty firm ideas about what our "live" retirement schedules might look like. While we won't be working on formal, written schedules -- heavens, we had enough of that in the office! -- we will be trying to visualize how our own retirement schedules might appear. This will not be difficult; we saw enough of them while we were working.

In this drill, we will call our schedules *notional*. We use the word notional because we are not looking for any written schedules. We just want to know, generally, what such schedules might look like. To help us think through this development, we'll actually peruse some of my own "live," *notional* retirement schedules. From here, you should be able to mentally see your own schedules just over the horizon.

Taking Care of Honey-Do's

When we first retire, we are likely to have a pretty long list of backlogged household chores, work that is in the deferred maintenance category. Facetiously, some people call these their "honey-do" list -- things that our "honey" wants done and says we *must* do. They are things that we may have put off doing, things that did not have to be taken care of right away, but things that someday must be handled. When we retire and find that we have a little more time -- like now -- we no longer have the excuse to defer taking care of these chores.

To help you jangle your own memory about what may be on your honey-do list, let's quickly take a look at mine. When I retired, I found the following were backlogged: repaint the inside of the garage, caulk around the roof chimney, expand the attic walkway, plant some new shrubs along the rear fence, remodel the exercise room, fix the plumbing in all bathroom toilets, and shop for a new car.

Of course, our honey-do lists will never be totally exhausted. Each week that passes brings additional tasks that must be done. Things as mundane as mowing the yard, raking the leaves, and planting the garden show up. Some of these chores must be done fairly early, either by ourselves or others. If they are not taken care of, they may constrain our "play days" -- our retirement fun days. We don't want that to happen.

In our "appealing things" inventory, we needn't put down any of the long-term chores from our "honey-do's." However, it is a good idea to provide time up front to take care of this initial work, so we can move along with our retirement planning.

Inventory of Appealing Things

The Preliminary List

This is probably the most crucial step in the process. Here we want to slow down to a snail's pace and find out *what we really like to do or want to do*. As with a lot of things, this may be easier said than done. We must very seriously ask ourselves what we really love in life. What kinds of things motivate us and make us happy? Remember that time is no longer an obstacle. Now it's an ally, a friend. The task at hand is to come to a dead stop and ask ourselves what kinds of things in life we really adore doing.

For instance, we could start by simply thinking about doing more of the same things we've liked doing in the past but had to "squeeze in" because we didn't have enough time to do them fully. Some examples that quickly coming to mind are: playing more golf, spending more time at the bridge table, rummaging around antiquing, getting more involved with gardening, going fishing more often, catching up on reading, exploring new avenues, or maybe even getting more sleep and resting-- whatever. A good starting point is to very carefully **list those top things in your life that you no longer want to be without**.

For now, let's call this our preliminary list. When we look back at this list later, we might realize that one or two of the things on the list could easily and joyfully monopolize the entire day. In our quest for variety, however, we really might not want to do that anyway. Just think how many people we know who retire, move near a nice golf course, and play golf nearly every day -- for three or more hours at a whack. How much of their day is left over? By the time they get up, get organized, play their round (or rounds) of golf, and return home, there are only a few hours of the day left. Of course, such a routine may sound appealing to some, but it is not for all of us. Even for these avid golfers, there are still enough vacant hours left in the day to accommodate a few, new, fun things too.

At this stage, we should take plenty of time to develop a *long* list. If something sounds as though it might be appealing and we'd like to do it, then we should put it down. We should just concentrate on adding to the list. Let's not be concerned about how to fit in each of our favorites at this point. That comes later.

Are you writing your list? I surely hope so. I hope this finds you sitting there with your pad scribbling down (or hammering out on your computer) your own list of "appealing things."

Adding to the Preliminary List

Even though we may have already covered nearly all of our hobbies in our preliminary list, it is a good idea now to pause and be sure that we have included them all. As we think about our hobby list, let's try to think through the entire range of intellectual, cultural and artistic experiences -- anything appealing that will keep our hearts and minds happily alive and kicking could qualify.

We might even embrace those things we haven't done for a while but might really like to get around to doing. At this point, we should also add those activities that we just might like to pursue as hobbies, even if we may have never tried them and are still a little uncertain. What we are really doing now is building a list of new activities that could become our new hobbies. Eventually, as we try them, we might be pleasantly surprised that some end up being our true favorites, overtaking some of our long-standing hobbies.

As we continue adding and thinking, thinking and adding, we should not be rushed. We've got to give ourselves plenty of time so we can carefully think through our own hobby list. If something didn't make the first cut when we started our list, it might be added now. Here are some additional examples: swimming, jogging, bicycling, playing tennis (or racquet ball), hunting (hmm!), skeet shooting (hmm, again), writing, painting, becoming more computer proficient, playing a musical instrument, singing in the church choir, auto mechanics, home shop work and photography.

Now, as a final test for inclusion, we should be sure to list other things we know we can do and that attract us, but that we've usually avoided because of the earlier time constraints. The only caution in adding any item is to be sure that each thing we add has the potential for being *totally satisfying*, in and of itself. Again, we're not talking about spending all our time on any one thing, but if it's listed here and now, it must have a good chance of delivering happiness and satisfaction. *That's the acid test.*

Still Other Favorite Things Considered

We called the initial inventory of "appealing things" our preliminary list. To that list we added our hobbies. You would think that as careful as we've been that we wouldn't have missed anything. However, when we now look back over our revised list so far, chances are good that we'll still see that we've missed one or two things. This especially applies to the simple things of life.

Take reading the daily newspaper, for instance. How many times do we ever really *read* the newspaper from cover-to-cover and relish all the stories and reports inside? We're not talking about the usual quick scan of the headlines after breakfast on the way to work. Yes, I know on the weekend, we used to read "all of the news," sometimes. Now, we can do it every day of our life, with fulfilling enjoyment -- if we think we might like it.

How about magazines -- reading some that we've avoided because of lack of time? (Since we've already covered reading in general, I hope that reading books is already listed -- if it suits you.)

How about television -- watching the tube? For some of us, this would have a very low priority; for others, it might be high on the list. Some might find that they've missed many, many favorite programs in the past, again because of time constraints. What about the late-night TV shows (such as Jay Leno and David Letterman). How about mid-morning shows (such as Regis and Kathy Lee on CBS, or early news coverage on CNN). We might want to make room for a few of these.

How about listening to more good music? There is now time to do that, too. Just watch the satisfaction level each one delivers; that will be the guide.

We've already covered the absolute requirement for *physical exercise* and maintaining our physical fitness, so if you've not yet listed exercise, you ought to add it now to your list. You'll definitely need to schedule several workout periods each week. You might also want to add your own *daily devotion period* (study time or morning meditation -- call it what you like). If it is important to you and you want to make room for it, now is the time to list it.

Break Pattern Excursions

Still rounding out the list and making a final check to assure that we haven't overlooked anything, we could now consider what we might call *break pattern excursions*. By this is meant unrushed, other activities that could be held on standby status when and if we need them. These can be used as fillers or to break the general routine of any seemingly monotonous trends that could develop. They are especially handy during bad weather days. As mentioned earlier, we certainly need to make way for variety as we develop our patterns and schedules.

Some of these break pattern excursions could consume several hours -- maybe even days or weeks. Here we are thinking about such things as visiting shopping centers; browsing the countless new books, magazines and papers at the libraries and book stores; strolling through the museums and art galleries; going to the theater; traveling or vacationing (short and long trips included); and even visiting with friends and loved ones (including the grand kids). We could also add that side trip to the beach or the mountains. This would be especially important if we have the resources for a vacation home.

The key to this drill, really, is to break the daily, weekly, and monthly routines. We want to assure that we have ample opportunity for providing plenty of variety and giving ourselves an occasional change of pace. A periodic reminder of our objective is helpful. We want to be able to fully enjoy retirement and never, never get bored or restless in living our retired life. If we do things right, we should be so busy that we never have time to get bored — period!

Finally, many friends of mine find happiness in *volunteer work*. This is a good time to consider that for ourselves, too. We probably never had much time to get involved with volunteer work before. Now the time might be right and the rewards plentiful. Examples are church-work, lodges and associations, civic league jobs, welfare assignments that benefit the needy and disadvantaged. There are many, many organizations needing volunteers. Folks running these places warmly accept additional help from any and all sources. Again, though, we must be sure that this sort of thing delivers satisfaction in our own life and meets our own desires and aspirations.

What If Our List Is Pretty Short?

Before concluding our work here to develop a list of "appealing things," let's ask one last question. What happens if our list is pretty short? Despite trying to develop a long list as we thought through our favorite things, we may have tossed most nominees aside. Maybe, at the time, they did not seem to meet the acid test of delivering happiness.

It may be that when we were working, some of us were genuine "workaholics." Perhaps you were married to one and found that you had little time for anything else. Bluntly put, workaholics and their spouses just never find many off-line things very appealing. All of us know a lot of people who have never played golf. They never found the time. Some even chide those who are foolish enough to knock a little white ball around in the grass. Others have never gone fishing or played cards or read good books. Still others are bored with museums and don't like shopping centers and grocery stores. They don't mind visiting relatives but are ready to leave shortly after they unpack their suitcases. These folks are the ones who just *loved* working. When they took vacations in the past, they were often anxious to get back to work. They called home or the office each day (sometimes several times a day) to see what was happening in the "real world" back there. This group may have just pooh-poohed each of the earlier suggestions about what might be some of their favorite and appealing thing to do. Are these folks (the workaholics and their spouses) hopeless? Should they just give up and go back to work? *Heck, no!* They succeeded at work, becoming workaholics, because they gave their jobs 100%, and so did their spouses. Some of the other things in life may have been missed because our workaholics were just *too engaged* at work. I know. That sort of thing also happened to me. I am a little bit like that, too. Maybe we all have some streak of the workaholic in our bones.

But here's the good news: for this group, there are opportunities galore to change direction and embrace new horizons. If those in this group think long enough and hard enough, they, too, can find things that are appealing. Then, when (and if) they concentrate on their retirement, they should find that they can embrace each new activity with the same intensity and vitality that they devoted to work during their employment years. They could even enjoy higher levels of happiness in retirement as well, because they will be putting their usual 100% into it.

Again, for us all, the real key is finding something out there that we really want to do, and if we stop and think about it carefully enough, I believe we can. We should really have a surplus of fun things to do, because unquestionably, there are plenty of things to do out there. Our job is to find those which offer the maximum degree of personal satisfaction and happiness. We should all be able to agree, too, that the human animal, intelligent man, was not made to be solely a work beast.

A Glance at a "Live" Example

While you are taking one last look at your own "appealing things list," you might want to peek at mine. It is attached as APPENDIX 1. This is a "live" list. I developed it using the same process we have just covered together. On my list you will see some of the things that my wife and I found appealing. As we worked our list, we tried to build a long list. That's why some of the things on our list (like your own) are naturally more appealing than others.

Let's say, for now, that we all have *our very own* "List of Appealing Things." Using the list should help us plan our own fun days, weeks and months as we continue now to the next chapter and build our plan.

5

BUILDING YOUR OWN RETIREMENT PLAN

WE are now going to "walk through" a systematic approach to building your own, satisfying, retirement plan. Remember, this will be a plan which will help you spend your days, weeks, and months doing only the things you want to do.

A Systematic Approach

Let's start with your own unique "appealing things" list. Keep your list before you. By now you should have your own favorite things pretty well fixed in your mind. Next, with your own list in front of you, keep mine handy too (the list in APPENDIX 1). We'll occasionally refer to both.

Now turn to APPENDIX 2 and quickly leaf through the various charts. You will see several notional schedules of my own for all kinds of conditions. You'll first see a typical daily schedule for *good weather* on *typical fall or winter days*

(APPENDIX 2-1). Look at the activities on this schedule very closely and compare them with my "favorite things" list (APPENDIX 1). Note that the activities on the schedule come directly from the list that I developed initially. You'll see, as you would expect, that certain events logically repeat themselves, in nearly every kind of weather condition. For my own schedule, that applies to early morning coffee, the daily workout, and the morning devotional.

Note, too, on this first chart (APPENDIX 2-1) that these good weather days provide an opportunity to get out of the house for exercise -- walking, strolling, and doing the things that one likes to do in nice weather. As you continue reviewing this schedule, occasionally glance back at my favorite things list. You should quickly see how this list of activities transplants itself into my "real world" schedules.

Let me reiterate that the schedules you are reviewing in APPENDIX 2 are not firm schedules in the usual sense. Earlier we called them notional schedules. As explained earlier, this means that nobody is suggesting that you develop and follow any rigid schedules. That sounds too much like work and resembles the kind of regimen we often were required to follow during our working years. To heck with that! We have graduated! But, still, I believe it is important for you to map out (at least in your mind) some pretty good ideas about how you want to spend your days. That will assure that you will be doing only the things that you want to do and that you are planning enough activities to keep you busily engaged throughout the day. This will insure that your days pass pleasantly without a trace of boredom, ever.

When you first look at my *notional* schedules and charts in APPENDIX 2, just remember that they are not rigid and should be used only as a guide. My wife and I may plan our days, weeks, and months fairly carefully, but we *rarely* make firm, written schedules. We keep notes and reminders to assure that we don't miss anything important. However, we firmly refuse to be driven by any kind of schedules -- even our own.

We sometimes even like to "trick" ourselves. We plan something during the week (or month), and as the event time approaches, we deliberately change directions -- abruptly cranking in something else we prefer to do. Occasionally we do this with little advance notice. We played this trick often when I first retired. It showed us (and all those observing) that we had *no* schedules or plans that could not be varied and changed at will. This quickly eliminated unwelcome calls from well-intentioned friends (and others) with requests to be at a certain place at a certain time. If we wanted to, we did; if we didn't, we would not. It was as simple as that!

As you continue looking at our schedules, you should spot something else. Our schedules are deliberately packed -- *loaded* with activities and things to do. We'd rather scrub some things along the way than not have enough to do. This is why we honestly can report to our friends who ask us what we are finding to do in retirement that we have never been busier -- or happier!

Before we jump ahead, try using the same review and critique process with the remaining schedules in APPENDIX 2. As you check these schedules (remembering that all of them are *notional*), occasionally glance back at my activities list (APPENDIX 1) and note how the activities were extracted from that list. Also, note how some repeat in many schedules. The reasons will be obvious. Watch, too, for changes which add variety and promote a change in pace.

As you continue reviewing the schedules, you will see an additional schedule for bad weather in the fall and winter. You'll also spot good and bad weather days for the spring and summer. These days are not so hard to fill, because the weather promotes more things to do, at least for most of us. The task, here, was just to be sure to cram in all the outside fun things so that nothing gets neglected and that our days remained packed.

Finally, as you check the remaining schedules, you will see a monthly chart and an annual, long-range calendar, illustrating how to assure that important events and activities will not be forgotten. You will also notice that, on all the charts and schedules, all of the activities and events come directly from my own master list of "appealing things." They are simply worked in to fit the weather, the time of year, the various claimants for time, and other conditions.

Other Considerations

By now, I hope, you see the process very clearly and are ready and anxious to embark on your own planning. There are still a few additional considerations before you tackle this. First, to assure that you provide sufficient planning time, it is usually best to map out the long range part of your plan first. Some activities require considerable advance planning. For instance, an overseas trip may require a lot of preliminary research as to the best airlines and hotels (vacancies, rates and booking procedures). The same goes for activities while you are there -- such as restaurants, shows and sightseeing. If one doesn't think through these trips sufficiently in advance, something might be missed. It's good also to plan important, periodic (maybe recurring) meetings well ahead. They have to be "blocked in" so you won't miss them.

Another timely suggestion: make your plans fit the weather and other variables. You will recall from my own notional schedules in APPENDIX 2 that I showed plans for all kinds of weather and seasons. This should help you think through your own schedules. The point is, you don't want a day to arrive (or week or month for that matter) and have it find you unprepared if the weather suddenly sours. That is where the "appealing things" list again comes in so handily. We can always, always, find other things to plug the gap. You will note that on my own notional schedules (in APPENDIX 2), it was not possible, or even desirable, to cram in all of my favorites from my list in APPENDIX 1. This left a lot of *residual favorites* to fill any gaps that might occur.

During your own planning, don't forget to include *recurring* household chores and housework, mundane as they may seem during your planning. If we neglect them now, they can monopolize some (or all) of our days later. It is best to work them in early -- giving priority to the really fun things on the list. (On my own schedules in APPENDIX 2, you'll see recurring household chores that were included.)

You may find it well to plan whole days to do home chores. An example is when I have to groom the yard or rake the leaves. By setting aside a day or so, this frees up larger blocks of time for our genuine *fun things*. (Again, you will see certain home chores blocked in for a whole day (or days), when appropriate.)

Another word of advice: as you plan *any* one week or month, be sure you are *truly* enjoying yourself. If you have any doubts, something is not going right. Your *fun things* should occupy the greater part of your life, and they must, individually and collectively, be delivering true satisfaction and total happiness all the time.

That's why frequent check ups are the order of the day. It is totally possible that your own "appealing things" list will have to be modified to add other, new activities that you find along the way. Some of the things that originally seemed to be totally appealing might now be found to be lacking, so they'll have to be dropped.

Don't be upset, or surprised, either, if you have to change your list and your plans slightly as time progresses. On the other hand, don't expect to have to do this. You might pleasantly find that you are very happy with your first cut plans. Simply do what you feel comes naturally and enjoy your happy days.

Permit me, once again, to stress variety. In any of your plans, be sure to *include variety* and some *change of pace*. As we've said earlier, one of the major causes for boredom is the repetition of things to the extent that they eventually become stale and boring. Unfortunately, this may even apply to doing some of the things we really liked to do, initially. If we do them too much or too long, they, too, tend to become stale. By deliberately adding some variety and dramatically changing the pace of activities, we can avoid getting into that rut. This is important. I've seen people get bored and into a rut without even knowing it. Check up often and see how happy, engaged and satisfied you really are.

While we are speaking of getting into ruts, use some care to assure that your schedules, either notional or otherwise, do not drive *you*. Be sure you drive *them*. One way to test this is to try the "trick yourself" routine in your own life. One day, deliberately change your plans without much notice. You will be showing yourself (and others) that you are totally in charge and also are ultra flexible to boot! This should bring you immediate satisfaction.

Early in the planning process, another technique is to scrap anything that tends to make you uncomfortable. As you put your plan into action, I believe it will be obvious whether your daily retirement activities are comfortable. If you find, for some reason, that you are not comfortable with your daily activities and they, unfortunately, are *not fun things,* then change them. Go back to your "appealing things" list and try again.

Finally, let me share with you a rather unique planning tool my wife and I have found helpful as we work our own daily schedules and plans. We *generally* know what we want to do during a given week or month because we have been talking and thinking about it. We may even have some pretty detailed notes or rough schedules if upcoming events are pretty important. However, to really firm up our daily schedule, we nearly always use our "in bed morning coffee sessions" to solidify our plans for the day.

At some point during our early day conversations one of us will say, "O.K., what are we going to do today?" -- or, "Let's plan our day." Then we usually, jointly, unravel the activities for the day. Sometimes we back up or revise earlier, tentative plans right on the spot to make way for late breaking events. Or maybe we change plans made yesterday because of weather conditions today. This final, early morning conference really helps us plot our day and confirm what we will really be doing the rest of the day. When we get up from our early morning coffee, we generally know what the day has in store and what is going to happen from morning until night. You might like trying this technique in working your own retirement plan.

At this point, I hope, you have some very solid ideas about how your days, weeks and months will play out. Your days should mostly be planned -- at least in your mind.

The best thing to do now is *just do it.*

6

LIVING YOUR
RETIREMENT PLAN

N OW, let's consider what happens when we really start to live our retirement plan. This is the fun part and something we've been looking forward to. As we start living our Golden Days, we want to watch for anything that could mar our plans or spoil our fun. This chapter discusses a few things to watch for to be sure that your happy days are not sidetracked in any way.

Keeping Track of Your Health -- Keep Going Forward!

Regardless of our health condition, we need to keep close track and do all we can to be sure we continuously go forward. Here I am speaking, not only of good physical health, but good mental health as well. As we've discussed, good health really helps promote a good, positive outlook and postures us to enjoy each hour of each day. Unfortunately, the opposite is also true. We have to be watchful and to know where we stand.

We have already made a solid commitment to do all we can to attain and maintain an optimum level of good health. Here are some suggestions for steps that can make good health a lasting reality.

You can, and should, continue listening to your body. It will tell you when you are feeling well and when you are not. Although there is a real danger in thinking or saying too much about our bodily conditions, we can all be alert for signals. Often when these signals appear, we can get back on track by strategies as simple as getting more rest or a little more exercise.

Sometimes we may deliberately depart from our established schedules for a short period, taking life at a more leisurely pace. Furthermore, while we are watching our health situation, I believe we should avoid letting the body totally dictate our future. By this I mean that we should become the masters of our fate (and body), not the other way around, if at all humanly possible. In any event, we *must not* go backward. We want to maintain our health.

We should keep a fairly close eye on our *weight and diet.* You've probably observed that sometimes the extra free time you enjoy in retirement can bring added pounds and inches around the midriff. This is normal. There is more time to look at good food and to try it. Now with a more leisurely pace, some of our friends may also entice us with glorious temptations as we more frequently share dining tables. In addition, our body metabolism works as an adversary. It tends to slow down with the aging process. Therefore, the earlier advice about watching our calories and fat intake continues to apply, perhaps even more stringently, as we proceed down the retirement trail.

Let's return to exercise again for a moment. We have

extensively discussed exercise and physical work-outs, but they deserve to be mentioned again, this time from a little different perspective.

Yes, we should all commit ourselves to developing a sound, regular exercise pattern and sticking to it. Most of us can work our way into a fairly good program, but sticking with it is another matter entirely. How many people do you know who at one point or another will excitedly tell you about a new exercise program they have found? ... how much they enjoy it ... how much better they feel ... how they don't have to worry so much about gaining weight. Then, *Bingo!* -- shortly thereafter, many of these same people return to their old patterns of inactivity. They've found many excuses to regress. They were "temporarily sick." They "went on an extended vacation and got out of the habit." They "saw some 'expert' who said they should 'take it easy'." We hear countless other "valid" reasons. All of these "excuses" have one thing in common. They stem from a genuine lack of resolve and commitment to stay with the program. Too soon, people forget how good they felt when they were vigorously engaged in their exercise programs and how their healthy, well-exercised bodies helped them nurture a better mental outlook.

Therefore, we must be determined to stick with our exercise program, and once we've found the right program, we must *stay with it --forever!* Sure, we may have to make changes to our programs, but we must commit ourselves to regular workout periods and go the limit that our bodies will allow.

Staying Motivated

Since we worked hard to begin our retirement with the *right frame of mind,* we should now make a deep commitment to keep this healthy, positive outlook -- to stay motivated. This should not be hard to do, because once we experience the happiness and the real fun of retirement, truly enjoying our Golden Years, there should be increased joy with each passing day.

A trusted friend of mine calls this "living with a golden attitude." I believe, too, that we will learn that we, ourselves, are largely responsible for having this good outlook on life. There are always good things happening all around us. Our job is to be watchful and mindful of these good things and to expect them to happen to us in our own lives. I've found that if we watch for good sufficiently, there won't be time or opportunity to observe much else. Good will certainly start to happen and continue happening!

The same good friend mentioned above has another favorite saying that I have come to love dearly. It is this slogan: "Stay Alert -- Stay Alive!" This thought is closely related to the one of attitude and staying motivated. Here my friend means *being alert* to the many good things we are seeing and experiencing. He also means we should avoid being aligned with those negative aspects we may encounter that can bring only gloom and doom. If we somehow can develop the habit of adhering to this slogan, the payoff will be great. We'll be alert and we'll stay alive, in the strictest and most literal sense.

Keeping the Right Outlook About Aging

We have already looked at some of the pitfalls of dwelling on the negative and the seeming declining status of man as the aging process continues. I hope it is now a little clearer why we should think, act, and associate with *progression* -- not regression. Even though we may all agree about the benefits of a *good outlook*, this may be very hard to attain (and maintain), if we do not posture ourselves properly. I'm convinced (because I've tried it) that anybody who emphasizes the positive, looks for beauty and good health, shares tales of *good news,* and spends little time on the opposites, is rightly postured. All of this helps a person get the most from each minute of every day.

One simple way to compound our successes is to associate with the right people -- people who are healthy themselves and have good, positive attitudes. These are the people we should hold up as our models, and, as we've said, there are plenty of them out there. To a great degree, we all make the choice in selecting our friends and associates. When we select happy, progressive and healthy ones, we're likely to find that some of this *goodness* rubs off on us. Put another way, we may be looking at models of what we, ourselves, might like to be. With sufficient emphasis, concentration and commitment, we can be those models!

Earlier we discussed the therapy of being around younger people. A friend of mine recently became our church nursery attendant. She had not been around very young children for a long time and initially expressed some reluctance in taking on the job. However, in two or three weeks, she was right into the swing of things and confided, "I've never been so happy in all my life -- watching after and taking care of these young people -- just observing their antics and happiness. I'm learning more from them than I'm teaching!"

The happy, fresh and enthusiastic views we get from young people spread and rub off. We'll no doubt get a healthy dose ourselves. Around younger people, we'll find that our thoughts don't dwell on ourselves and our own problems so much. We won't look at ourselves so much as being old. Neither will those around us. Haven't you seen an older person with such vibrant views, and who is so interesting, that you seldom (if ever) stop to think about that person's age? We all have seen them and may even be fortunate to know such people presently. If we are going to attain this happiness and acquire these refreshed views about aging, we've got to place ourselves in a position to make that happen.

I have a friend who is 82 years young. He is an avid runner. About two years, he "graduated," as he puts it, and ran the marathon. He is very proud of that, but jokingly says, "It may be my first and my last marathon." We all know that running the marathon is not an easy feat![21]

When my friend is asked by others how he managed to do it, he tells them he only got to be a serious runner after retiring (about 15 years earlier). He goes on to say that with retirement he found that he had the time to devote to the things he really enjoyed. This included vigorous exercise and running. He obviously progressed up his "ladder of success" until he "graduated" to marathon status.

So far, we have been talking about physical prowess. Let's now turn for a moment from physical beauty to *total* beauty. For many years, I've been impressed at the real beauty of older (let's say aging) people. I know several retired, so-called "older folks" who just *radiate* with *inner beauty*. (Some are not so bad on the outside, either!) Let's take Dolores Hope, the beautiful and devoted wife of celebrity Bob Hope. After 62 years of marriage and at 87 years of age, she seems to become more glamorous with the passage of time. We can be thankful that we can think of countless other examples.

These personal examples give us genuine basis for becoming encouraged ourselves. They tend to show each of us that, with the proper approach, age can be expected to bring strength, well-being and *total* beauty, as well. This is a tough match for anyone -- youth included! So, Seniors, welcome to the new world of beauty!

Changing Some of Your Initial Plans

Let's say that you have started living your retired life. You are doing the things that you like to do and have found plenty of fun things to do. You are physically fit, have a great mental attitude, and have never been happier. All of this -- plus, you are totally beautiful. Then for one or a combination of reasons, you find your days (and maybe your weeks and even months) start to drag a little. Some of the things that you were doing are no longer as much fun. Maybe you've deliberately had to scrap or adjust some things. Now what?

Don't be surprised or disappointed if *a little* of this happens in your retired life. While your plan should be solid enough to carry you through and to avoid such occurrences, situations can change. Sometimes our tastes and desires, as well as our capabilities, change with the passage of time.

As discussed when we had just started to build our plans at the beginning of our retired lives, we should occasionally check up to see that our days are bringing *total* happiness. Caution: don't *expect* the negative! Your plans *probably* will be delivering total happiness. That is the way we designed them. However, you want to be the first to know if things start to lose their appeal, even slightly. This can signal the need to get busy and change your plan. Some of these changes may be temporary; some may be of longer duration.

Again, good news: changing our plans will not be hard if we have our handy-dandy set of alternatives, or substitute, *fun things* ready to go. Earlier we discussed the need to watch other people and ponder some additional activities we might want to have in our own lives. We talked about finding a few new fun things as well. At the time, these new things may not have had sufficient appeal to show up on our retirement plans. However, at a certain point -- like, now -- they might.

Therefore, if the need arises, plug them in and watch for good, positive results. When you become happy again (or totally happy again, we should say), then you are back on track. You have found the right combination again and are ready to continue living your happy days of retirement.

Just be sure, as you engage the new options and alternatives, that each one stands on its own. Each one must be able to deliver lasting, satisfying, happy experiences. If the new activity meets this test, it's in!

Enjoying Life and Making the Happy Times Last

If we are doing the things we really like and are enjoying each day of our retired life, it would take a miracle to pull us away from this life. Being human, though, it is only natural to ask if this happiness will really continue.

As we seriously consider the question, we may all arrive at the same answer. These days can continue -- on and on -- if we really want them to. This answer becomes even more plausible when we remember that each day is already bringing total happiness. We are now having the time of our lives in the prime of life.

Occasionally, it is well for us to remember the "old days" -- our days at work. When we now consider our true freedom -- relief from schedules, the commands and directions of others and other situations, we breathe sighs of relief. We see the real contrast between the two lives. This glorious retired life we are living now is the life to live!

All of this never has to change. We have very carefully prepared our retirement plan. We have made the necessary modifications and are ready to make others if and when required. We've got activities and fun things to do that are heavily backlogged. We wish we had time to do more of these things, but we know that it would be impossible to get around to doing them all in one lifetime. We're so busy! We know that we will never, ever get bored. We are just busy doing the things that we enjoy. What a wonderful life!

Passing on The Good News

As you start living your own Golden Years and experiencing true happiness in retirement, no doubt you will often be questioned about your present status. Your friends might ask, "Why are you so happy?" "What do you find to do?" "How did you approach retirement?" Here comes the real joy: you can share all your good news stories with others. Then you can just sit back and watch them enjoy their Golden Days, too.

Do you remember, near the start of the book, that we noted how many people really feared retirement and were afraid that it was destined to bring days of gloom and doom? Now that we have started to live our happy days of retirement and know differently, this is our opportunity to share the secrets of how we found our own happiness.

The task is to tell our inquisitors -- our friends who are also interested in finding happiness in retirement -- a little about the steps we took and how we proceeded. We can start by telling them how we got mentally ready to have joy-filled retirement days. Then we can explain how we proceeded to develop a methodical plan -- our own unique plan to deliver happiness in retirement.

We need to review the total process. We need to explain how we carefully developed our own list of "appealing things"-- how we incorporated this list into our retirement plan. Then we can follow by relating some of our happy experiences and sharing some of our own success stories. As we do this, it will be a joy to see them engage their own retirement plans. Furthermore, I believe we will find a real boost to our own happy days as we help others find theirs, too. All we have to do is be alert for the opportunities to share, and then do it!

7

HANDLING THE ROUGH SPOTS

O NE would think, by now, that we had covered nearly all the bases. Although that is true, it would be well to call attention to a few other "real world" problems that could occur for some of us. That way, we'll be fully prepared -- just in case. Many of us may never have to face these problems. Others may, and some may have already crossed the threshold. Since "life must go on," we all want to be as prepared as we can. We don't want any surprises!

What Happens If Things Don't Go According to Plan?

After we retire, things may not always go according to plan. Let's examine two real possibilities --two circumstances that could really upset nearly anyone's plans.

[1] What if we lose our good health? We already know how hard it is to be truly happy without our health. What good is our plan if we can't live it? What do we do now?

Obviously, as we've said before, we try to get well fast. This is clearly our first and highest priority. We must naturally adjust any and all plans and activities to accommodate our new quest for regaining our health. Nothing else matters much. Exactly what we do and how we do it, of course, will depend upon the circumstances of the individual case. However, with some intense thought and more good planning, we should be able to meet the new challenges and find some happiness as well. It is clear, though, that we will have to change our plans and change our days. In making changes, we can (if we look hard and long enough) find new activities that can bring some measure of happiness and satisfaction. Finding and maintaining happiness will provide a natural, therapeutic effect as well. We'll be more likely to regain our health more quickly.

In finding these so-called new things, where better could we start than by returning (again) to our "favorite things" list? We may immediately find the right new activity or the right new activity or the right combination. At least, we should get some fresh suggestions to bridge the gap. This may not be easy, but we should be on the right track.

[2] What if our finances become "stretched?" Despite our earlier plans to be financially sound when we retire, it is still possible in these days clouded by economic uncertainty that we could become a little strapped. With good adjustment, we should be able to modify our lifestyles, including our retirement plans, to fit the ups and downs of most situations.

In severe cases, though, an obvious solution would be to get more income. Let's ask ourselves a few questions. First, where does this increased income come from? Are we going back to work? Will we rob a bank? This last question is posed to show the absurdity of both of the previous questions. We have already agreed that we are living the happy days of retirement. Why would we even consider working again, except in the most dire circumstances? Those who might suggest working "part-time" also are in for some surprises.[22] There are few jobs and positions for genuine executives where working anything but "full speed" will meet the demands of the business situation. If we agree to work "on a part-time basis," we will probably find that our working hours gradually start to expand. Soon our workday will resemble "full-time" work. We don't want that! Remember, we just graduated!

For middle level executives and working class people, part-time is also not too attractive. One rarely gets paid what he or she is worth, out there competing with the regular work force. In addition, ordinary work benefits, if any, usually go to the fully employed. While all of this may be considered "normal," why should we become *second class citizens?* It remains clear that we should resist returning to the work environment, unless we decide that is what we really want to do.

Then what is the answer? We are financially strapped! We have a possible crisis! Well, the answer may be fairly obvious. What we most need now is *better control of* the "demand side" of our lives. We've got to set more realistic limits on our expenses and make some real changes. One serious option might be to relocate. Most of us do not want to consider relocation when we retire, and we have a lot of company. Relocation expert Peter Dickinson says that "about 70 percent of us retire in the place we now live," and that "of those who move, about 20 percent move to a smaller place in the same general area -- only about 10 percent actually leave their home state."[23] Yet our financial situation might require us to consider moving to another location which takes less money for living. We know that some places are more expensive than others, so relocation might be the answer. This could make a real difference in our overall retirement expenses.[24]

If you pursue the relocation option seriously, you might not have the foggiest idea about where you would want to move. You'll be moving primarily to save money, but there are so many other factors to consider: health and climate, safety and security, cultural conditions, social aspects (the people and the surroundings), proximity to other friends and relatives, and lifestyles, just to mention a few. If you have absolutely no idea of where you might want to move, you could consider some of the "most desirable" locales.

There are lists of cities that are prepared by people who make extensive studies of all factors in the area. The cities on these lists change from year to year and vary from researcher to researcher. It may surprise you, though, to learn that many of the same cities appear on the lists of nearly each one of those who do extensive research. To give you an example of recent "top cities" on one prominent researcher's list, here is Norman D. Ford's top five: 1) Boulder, Colorado (because this is "the ultimate health and fitness town"); 2) Eugene, Oregon ("combines the relaxed air of academia with the high energy of a major health center"); 3) Ann Arbor, Michigan (cited for repeated awards as a "safe, clean, family oriented place to live"); 4) Madison, Wisconsin ("... an astonishing beautiful city full of friendly people..."); and 5) Chapel Hill, North Carolina ("An exquisite college town" with all the trimmings).[25]

In reviewing any "top listing" by the researchers, many of us would ask: "Why would anybody choose 'City X,' or 'City Y?'" In the final analysis, it all depends on how we weigh the various factors. What appeals to one would not necessarily appeal to others. However, any top listing might be a good starting place.

While up to now, our retirement plan was developed without regard to location, if we get really serious about relocating, we might now have to return to the proverbial "square one" -- i.e., we may have to start all over. A new locale could impact drastically our whole retirement plan. We might quickly find that several activities, which we had planned and looked forward to, are not available at the new location. Still, there may be some things available at our new residence that were not considered previously. Even if the new location precludes some of our favorite activities, however, if it brings us substantial financial gain and relief, we might have to entertain moving.

Whether we relocate or take other abrupt steps to reduce our retirement expenses, we should still be in for some good news. With the amount of thought we've given retirement planning, we should be able to take our retirement plan and, for most cases, make the necessary revisions. Our revised plan must simply be tailored to meet the new circumstances.

This sounds easy, and in all but drastic cases, it really may be. However, the requirement now is to carefully review our standby list of appealing activities and select *only* those which require *modest resources*. We may also have to search for other, less expensive activities, depending on the situation.

Of course, there are practical limits to how far we can go with this approach. If our retirement income is too far out of line with our expenses, we have a real job on our hands. Not only may we have to consider relocation, but we may also have to resort to other, more drastic means as well.

A little more good news: as we start looking more closely for these more modestly priced activities and thinking about how to revise our plan, we should be in for some pleasant surprises. We should quickly find that there are increasing numbers of fun things to do that require little or no funds at all. Earlier in our planning, we probably overlooked, or tabled, some of these activities because we did not then have to consider them. They were outclassed, initially, by some other, more expensive alternatives that seemed to have more attraction (for the moment).

Let's examine some of these *low cost, no cost* options more closely. In an increasing number of cities, there are hefty *discounts for seniors*. Some theaters hold top-choice seats until the last minute, then the seniors get priority -- often for a song. Some department stores have regular senior discounts, and on certain days, some even have complimentary coffee and deserts for their older clientele. In addition, public transportation in many cities is greatly discounted, and many restaurants offer "early bird dinner specials." Local museums and art galleries also cater to seniors. Finally, there is likely to be more time for reading and visiting the book stores and libraries and for visiting friends and relatives. If we look long and hard enough, we can find some real bargains and new, exciting things to do.

Unless we have a genuine catastrophic situation on our hands, with our new discoveries, we should be able to update our plans and include more and more of these modestly priced activities in our daily affairs. The trick is just to crank up the grey matter and search for these new things. Once we've found them, we tailor our lifestyles and appetites to accommodate the new activity patterns. We might again be pleasantly surprised to see that our "revised retirement plan" becomes so attractive and satisfying that we want to stick with it even when our financial situation improves. We might find a lot of truth in the often repeated stories that "the best things in life are free."

Thus we see that even with the most adverse financial conditions, there is a solution, and we can retain our state of happiness in retirement.

Everything Goes Better in Pairs

If I could, this is one I'd just as soon sidestep, but that would not be fair to any of us. So, here goes.

About everything we have done or talked about doing so far addresses a person with a spouse -- man and wife. My own schedules in APPENDIX 2 were built with my wife and me in mind. Like our own lives, they were structured on a partnership basis. I'd quickly admit that a lot of the activities on those schedules would be meaningless trying to "fly solo."

We all realize, too, that many people are already living without their spouses. They have already learned by experience that their happy days of togetherness are "here today and gone tomorrow," as the old saying goes. On the other hand, for a relatively smaller number, some have never had a spouse or close partner; they have lived alone all the time. In ages 45-64, about one in four is either widowed, divorced, or has never been married.[26] In the 65 and older category, while over half of the people are married, about one in three lives entirely alone.[27] Our chances of flying solo are pretty high.

While we are speaking of this flying solo and what it might mean, there is another fact to consider. From strictly a *numbers* standpoint, did you ever stop to consider that each married person with a living spouse has about a 50% chance of living alone; i.e., either he or she will be the first to pass on, or that person will be left behind?[28] What then?

Since "life goes on," we must find a way to adjust, difficult as it certainly will be. While I have not crossed over that bridge yet (and may not, if I'm in the other 50%), let me suggest to the reader that we carefully analyze our options. What alternative choices do we have? For a moment, let's carefully reflect on others that we have seen in this situation. How do they make it? Let's especially concentrate on those surviving spouses who are happy and well-adjusted (or seem to be). We may want to target them as our new model. Let's ask ourselves how they spend their days. What things do they do? As we consider alternatives, some might slowly start to surface and appear feasible in our own lives. That's what we're looking for. If you are in the group who is already living alone, remember that our analysis of choices may be especially appealing to you. You are already there! However, even you may need a boost and a change.

Using our own observations, analyses and studies of others, let's look at some possible alternative choices.

1. One could endeavor to *find another spouse* -- and fast! How many people do you know out there who were so very happily married for such a long time that you just knew that he or she would never marry again, no matter what? Then, fairly shortly after the spouse passed on, *boom!* -- there was a wedding. The new couple looked like true lovebirds; never had either seemed so happy! Wow! Were we surprised? Well, you know, we should not have been.

It is not terribly unusual that the surviving spouse, cut adrift from the happiest and most loving of marriages, is the most attracted to getting married again. These people like married life, and doing things with a partner is their natural drift. Therefore, *if* (and this is a big if) the right partner comes along, it seems fairly normal to try to find happiness again, as a married person. For many this will work -- if they can find that right person!

2. Other people might deliberately want to "go it

alone." (I'd like to think I'm in that category, and my wife will love me for it!) People in this group found their days together so very special and endearing that they do not want to tarnish any of their precious memories. Another person would really interfere.

My wife and I had a dear friend who was happily married for nearly fifty years. He and his wife were together almost constantly; they were a team in every respect. Each exuded love, especially when they were around each other. Their marriage was a true, continuing love affair of the highest order.

When this dear friend's wife passed on, he still treasured her companionship, of course in an entirely different context. His house was adorned with her pictures and things and keepsakes that seemed to breathe her presence. In the winter, he vacationed in Florida for a month, spending that time at the same hotel and in the same suite that he and his wife had enjoyed for more than 30 years. We ran into him a couple of times in Florida while we were vacationing. There he had dinner in "their favorite restaurant," still with two chairs at "their" small, candle-lit table. Management was very accommodating. During the daytime, he went for long walks on the beach where every nook and turn along the way brought him precious memories.

He also had a summer cottage in Maine. Friends nearby said he exhibited the same types of patterns when he vacationed there. Now, the bottom line. This friend was very happy living with his memories. More than once he confided that he would not be happy with any other person as a spouse. Of that I am quite sure. For him, this second alternative was the preferred choice.

3. One might link up with a buddy (or a pal) -- or maybe a series of buddies or pals. I have known many people who have done so. This new, close association may have started out fairly slowly. These new pals found they had much in common. Maybe they had both lost their spouses recently. They probably shared common interests, also. With more time now, they may have played a little more golf during the week -- or gone fishing a little more often. This newly found friend rounded out the agenda, filling it with all kinds of things to do -- sometimes new and often very satisfying things.

In the process, this friendship deepened, along with the extended periods of being together with this pal. Soon, the relationship seemed to fill (or almost fill) that very real void that was left not so long ago.

This type of choice maintains many of the characteristics of the second option. There is still time to savor and treasure the memories of a dearly departed spouse. The newly developed relationship with a friend makes a reasonable compromise. If we think about it, I'm sure that many of us can recall several people we know who have embarked in this direction.

4. Some, when faced with the drastic reality of having lost a spouse, become intensely involved in *volunteer activities.* Several of my friends have chosen this option. My own church (fortunately for all of the members) finds several such individuals at the helm of volunteer activities. Many are preoccupied and even consumed with this newly found engagement. Others I know become allied with various charitable institutions -- some full-time and some part-time. The welcome mat is always out from these types of agencies. The volunteers do much good for their communities and for their fellow man. This is a noble undertaking, and it consumes great amounts of time -- nearly every hour that one is willing to give. Such engagement can offer rich personal rewards and satisfaction.

5. One might relocate to a retirement home. In a retirement community, we can find ample opportunity for socializing, companionship and affection. These are the real voids and the things we yearn for most when we lose our spouse.

Eventually moving to a retirement home will probably hold great promise for each of us, even if it doesn't at the moment. However, it always depends on the individual; one has to be ready for it. Suffice it to say that this option may be near the top of the list for many of us.

6. One might even start up a small business. Hold it, now! I thought we had already made a strong case for *never* working again! Why, then, would we entertain this option?

I'll admit that this is an option to be considered only in the most drastic of circumstances. However, what happens after a reasonable period of time, if a person continues to find life totally unbearable without a spouse? No matter what he or she may try or do, they find themselves consumed by prolonged grief. Let's say this person also has a ready hobby or high-demand skill that might blossom into a new, small-scale business. Let's also assume that our person recognizes the prospects of controlling the new venture so that it doesn't get out of hand and mean the total end of retirement. Sound attractive? For some, it might be appealing under such dire circumstances.

7. One might consider getting a pet or spending more time with a pet one already has. I realize that one really should be a pet lover to make this option attractive, but I have friends who could seemingly spend eternity caring for, and being with, their pets. I am sure their pet friends bring real companionship.

I've known a lot of people who had never had a cat or

a dog, but when they tried it, they found great happiness. That is why I believe this option certainly merits listing, as a major option to be considered. Of course, our hours and our days will pass in direct proportion to the amount of time we find this new, close relationship with our pet (or pets) satisfying.

8. A final approach might be what we would call _a combination_. Here I mean combining one or more of the other options. The isolation of each option, initially, was done to help us discern the individual appeal of each one. Now let's think about putting several together.

As we look back at the choices, we will realize that they are not mutually exclusive. Some combine nicely with others. For example, a person could develop a pretty close relationship with a buddy and spend a lot of time with that close friend. Simultaneously, that person could get a new pet and also do volunteer work, depending on available time. This combination method is more than likely what we'd really be doing with our lives anyway, as we march down the adjustment trail.

Regardless of which option, or options, we employ, we should realize that _change is the order of the day._ No matter which particular retirement plan we developed jointly with a given spouse and embarked upon initially, our activities and our plans must now change.

Fortunately, we remain well postured for the task. This would be the time that we would thoroughly review all that we have learned about doing our advanced preparatory work properly. We would continue by carefully analyzing and selecting attractive activities from our now maybe new "appealing things" list, methodically working them into our revised plans and monitoring results closely. Although this second time around is likely to be much more difficult at the outset, we should all be well equipped to make the required revisions to our original plans. As with other times in our lives when we have found change arise, we should be able to make the necessary modifications and proceed with living. If we do the job right, we should discover that we find continued happiness in retirement. That continues to be what it's all about even when the rough spots appear.

8

REAPING THE JOYS OF COMPANIONSHIP

THROUGHOUT this book we have examined the treasures and joys of retirement. We now realize that much happiness awaits us as we embark on our new, happy, retired lives.

We said that we would have more time to do the things that we really wanted to do. We would have time to pursue hobbies, maybe to look for new ones. Away from work, there would be time to relax and recharge. We saw, too, that we would be relieved from the burdens and pressures of the work place, with all the attendant frustrations and mental challenges.

We also knew that conditions for maintaining our physical and mental health would be improved. There would be more time for exercise, and we could be more serious about, and committed to, our regular workout programs. We recognized, too, that there would be more opportunity for spiritual growth -- for becoming a real friend with God. Yes, these are a few of the major treasures of retirement. Perhaps you can think of others.

Another that quickly comes to my mind is *companionship*. As with some of the other retirement treasures, this may be the greatest single jewel of them all. Man is, indeed, a very social animal, maybe more so than any other creature in the animal kingdom. Nearly every one of us dearly likes to be in the company of others. (Naturally, we like to be with some, more than others.) In this social mode, we can swap a few tales and reminisce. At the right time, we can even get a little boost to our egos. (We all need some of this from time to time.) We can listen to the other fellow's problems and know that while we are listening, this simple human act, alone, is bringing sizable relief and comfort to our friend.

These improved opportunities for companionship, offered by our new retired life, can also lead to developing stronger, more lasting relationships -- deeper love and affection. Among couples, for instance, it is very common to see some real, barn-burning romantic affairs rekindled. Ever watch a group of senior couples cuddling unhurriedly on the dance floor? Note the twinkle in their eyes. Love affairs might be the more accurate description of this rekindling. Back in the work mode, there was hardly time for a "smack on the cheek." Now, with nothing but time on their side, retired people can slow way down and really see the good things in each other. There's time to observe the countless good that the other person does. There's also time to see how truly lovely and beautiful a person has become -- both inside and out!

In the process of aging together, a retired couple has the time to share (in the truest meaning of the word). They can share their total life with each other. When things go well, there is ample time to share even the smallest of details. This kind of sharing sometimes makes even a seemingly small grain of happiness or joy *for one* suddenly turn into a giant harvest for *both*. We have all seen this countless times. Moreover, when adversity appears, there are time and opportunity to fight the battle together. Each is there to provide tender, nurturing care at those crucial moments when nothing else will suffice. For this, earth has no substitutes.

When we consider a couple living together in retirement, is there any reason why they should not find increased, meaningful joy in each other's companionship? Is there any reason, either, why a real-world love affair should not bloom and keep blooming? Hardly.

If there were not another blessing from retired life, this cultivation of a more loving life with a spouse -- the enrichment of companionship -- would make it all worthwhile.

What about the person living alone? Recall that many of us no longer have a spouse. Some of us were never married. Does retirement offer these people any opportunity to experience the increased joys of companionship? The answer is, of course, "Yes, most definitely."

Many of the things that apply to the retired couple apply equally to single retirees and to retirees who are surviving spouses. Being no longer tied to the grind of working, they have ample opportunities to cultivate close, caring, loving relationships with others. This would seem to apply especially to one or, possibly, two very close, intimate friends.

There is the opportunity to observe the true and good attributes of the other party and to really get to know and love that person. As with couples, there is time to share the good and bad days -- to be always there when needed. The opportunity to shoulder life's many joys and burdens together is still present. In the process, it is only natural and normal to find increased companionship and true affection.

With those two qualities, we've uncovered the truly magic words in living: *companionship and affection.* With them, we have everything. Without them, we stand alone. Having someone with whom to share your fondest memories and provide each other timely and mutual support is a real blessing. Most of us have found that "No man is an island, entire of itself..."[29] or, as a favorite song of the 1960's goes, "People who need people are the luckiest people in the world."

As we start our retired lives and continue to live them, we can and should expect to cultivate more companionship in our not-so-rushed lives. Added to our other retirement treasures, we will definitely find *real happiness* in retirement, in our *Golden Years.*

9

SUMMARY AND CONCLUSIONS

W E HAVE COVERED a lot of ground since we began our quest for happiness in retirement. We started by taking a closer look at retired people. We wanted to find out how much happiness retired life was bringing to them. We found that many are not truly happy and are still searching for the magic answers.

Next, we wanted to make sure that we, ourselves, felt it was not only possible, but probable, that we could find a happy, satisfying life in retirement. We went on to examine concepts and ways to assure that we had the right foundational thinking at the outset.

We reviewed how to get the right mental attitude about retiring and how to deal with the advancing years. We called this the cornerstone of our foundation. Next, we considered some of the things to watch out for and how to guard and guide our thinking. We also discussed at some length three other desirable foundation blocks: getting ready financially, attaining good health and staying that way, and keeping close to God (probably the key to it all). We were then ready to embark on building our plan.

Initially we examined scores of appealing activities. I then asked you to take your own activities and build them into your specially tailored list of "appealing things." You next viewed this list from several different angles to assure that it was complete and rounded out. Then you tried to build a *long* list of activities. Each item on the list was tested to assure that it would be able to deliver *true happiness.*

You took your own individual fun things, as we called them, and built them into your very own, unique, retirement plan. You started by taking your "appealing things" list and comparing it to my own live listing in APPENDIX 1. You continued by taking activities from your favorite things list and carefully working them into our own plan.

This led to reviewing what we called some of my *notional* schedules. These appeared in APPENDIX 2. You will remember, too, that when we talked about schedules, we emphasized the word *notional.* We wanted to label anything we saw as *type* schedules -- not firm, demanding, time schedules. (We vowed never again to follow any firm schedules. We left them all behind at work!)

After you built your own, individual plan, I asked you to consider several concepts about how to actually start *living your plan.* We recognized the importance of keeping track of our health and ever going forward. We also wanted to keep the right mental outlook, to stay motivated, all along the way. Then we gave considerable thought to revising our plans as circumstances change.

You became aware of how to use standby items from your "appealing things" list when revisions to your plan were required. We next discussed how to make these happy retirement days last and how to share them with others.

Recognizing the realities of living, we paused and examined what we called rough spots. We saw some of the things that might happen to upset our original plans. We investigated various means to overcome each obstacle in our path.

Finally, before we closed, we took one last look at companionship, a key ingredient of happiness, anytime and anywhere. We labeled this final look "Reaping the Joys of Companionship." Together, we explored various ways for improving our ties with our friends and loved ones. We recognized that retirement provides increased opportunities for enriching championship in our lives. We even proclaimed that by finding *companionship and affection,* we had uncovered the truly magic words in living. I hope you got the message, coming away with a renewed sense of the importance of loving others. In addition, we should have refreshed our commitments to listening to others and helping them.

As mentioned when we first started, the objective, for each one of us, was to build our own, unique, individual retirement plan -- a plan which would provide lasting happiness in retirement. Glancing back now, this should have happened. Each of us should have our own plan. It does not matter how *detailed or explicit* your own plan is. It matters little whether the plan is written out in great detail or whether it is simply fairly well fixed in mind. As long as each of us knows where we are and clearly where we are going, the result should be the same.

As we approach each day, month and year, we should be engaged (rather busily) in fun things -- carrying out activities that bring happiness, satisfaction, and total enjoyment throughout our retirement lives. If we hit rough spots, we should now be prepared to make adjustments and continue with our happy days.

Before we close, let's congratulate ourselves on this

pursuit. Let's also take one last look to see if we can highlight what we might call our "lessons learned" from this experience. You might like to call them your own special "secrets" to finding happiness in retirement. Let's list them:

1. Develop a close friendship with God. We list this first. It is the key to it all. We simply cannot make any mistakes when we get close to God and stay there.

2. Get (and keep) good thoughts every moment of every day. Armed with these good and right thoughts, we will stay motivated and experience the good that we really expect.

3. Remember to give high priority to daily exercise programs. Exercise keeps us fit and well postured for happiness -- in mind and body.

4. Try to keep the body's weight under control -- don't let it "creep" upward. Let's make a commitment to get (and stay) as trim as we can.

5. Watch the diet -- calories and fat intake. We "are what we eat," so let's vow to be vigilant.

6. Get plenty of rest. We want to give our bodies and minds a real chance to completely "recharge."

7. Watch how we look at "aging," becoming seniors. Remember that we can maintain our freshness and inner beauty (and outer "good looks") well into the future!

8. Let's be sure we are having lots of fun. We know how to cram our days with joy-filled activities. Let's just do it!

9. Let us vow that we will never "get into a rut" and risk getting bored. We will keep enough variety in our lives that we are constantly refreshed.

10. Above all, let's have a happy retirement. We know *how* and we promise to *do it!*

Best wishes to each of you, and may God bless you in your happy days of retirement.

APPENDIX

Appendix 1

Preliminary List
Appealing Things -- Things I Might Like to Do

- Get in the morning workout
- Set Daily Devotional period
- Play tennis
- Play golf
- Enjoy the computer
- Play the saxophone
- Go fishing
- Visit the vacation home often
- Have afternoon tea
- Visit kinfolks (grand kids)
- Do recurring home chores
- Visit museums and galleries
- Go to the theater or movie
- Attend church regularly
- Read some good books
- Listen to good music more
- Catch up on magazines
- Read more magazines
- Read the daily newspaper
- See a TV show at night
- Watch morning TV show
- Dine with friends often
- Visit shopping centers
- Weekend at local Resort
- Walk in the neighborhood
- Sightsee in Old Town
- Take on more church work
- Find more volunteer work
- Attend more prof. meetings
- Try writing a book
- Do some college teaching
- Learn to play the piano
- Do some car repairs
- Try Autocross or Car Meet
- Return to playing handball
- Take a trip on a cruise ship
- Visit Europe
- Visit the Middle East
- See the Near East
- Return to the Far East
- Join Univ. Advisory Board
- Go bicycling
- Try photography
- Take dancing classes
- Refresh on a foreign language
- Engage the Internet
- Make frequent library visits
- Learn household repairs
- Use home shop equipment
- Engage in civic activities
- Join a nature studies group
- Help youngsters find jobs
- Participate in politics
- Visit USA scenic attractions
- Revise photo albums, tapes
- Enjoy indoor swimming
- Learn to ski
- Beautify the garden
- Get a pool table
- Go bowling
- Try solitaire/cross-word puzzles
- Get and use a camper/ RV
- Get involved little league
- Get reacquainted with scouting
- Try Skeet shooting
- Play ping-pong
- Sing in Civic Song Club

Typical Fall or Winter Daily Schedule -- Good Weather

Monday	Thursday
8:30 AM - 9:15 AM -- Coffee, TV, read	8:30 AM - 9:15 AM -- Coffee, TV, read
9:15 AM - 9:45 AM -- Morning workout	9:15 AM - 9:45 AM -- Morning workout
9:45 AM - 10:15 AM -- Daily devotional	9:45 AM - 10:15 AM -- Daily devotional
10:15 AM - 10:45 AM -- Shower/ dress	10:15 AM - 10:45 AM -- Shower/ dress
10:45 AM - 11:30 AM -- Breakfast/read	10:45 AM - 11:30 AM -- Breakfast/read
11:30 AM - 1:15 PM -- Computer/chores	11:30 AM - 1:15 PM -- Computer/chores
1:15 PM - 1:45 PM -- Have light snack	1:15 PM - 1:45 PM -- Have light snack
1:45 PM - 3:30 PM -- Walk nearby	1:45 PM - 4:30 PM -- Stroll park/ town
3:30 PM - 4:15 PM -- Rest, read, nap	4:30 PM - 5:15 PM -- Rest, tea, read
4:15 PM - 4:45 PM -- Tea, read, TV	5:15 PM - 5:45 PM -- Computer, calls
4:45 PM - 5:30 PM -- Computer, calls	5:45 PM - 6:15 PM -- Happy Hour, TV
5:30 PM - 6:00 PM -- Happy Hour, TV	6:15 PM - 7:15 PM -- Dinner (longer ?)
6:00 PM - 7:00 PM -- Dinner (longer ?)	7:15 PM - 8:00 PM -- Chores, music
7:00 PM - 8:00 PM -- Chores, music	8:00 PM - 11:30 PM -- Read, TV, audio
8:00 PM - 11:30 PM -- Read, TV, audio	11:30 PM - 12:00 AM -- Read/TV in bed
11:30 PM - 12:00 AM -- Read/TV in bed	

NOTES: (1) The above daily type schedule is typical for fall or winter
days with *good weather* -- when we can still get outside and
enjoy it.
(2) These activities come right from our own listing of
"appealing things," Appendix 1. Naturally, your own list will
be quite different from mine.

Typical Fall or Winter Daily Schedule -- <u>Bad Weather</u>

Monday	Thursday
8:30 AM - 9:15 AM -- Coffee, TV, read	8:30 AM - 9:15 AM -- Coffee, TV, read
9:15 AM - 9:45 AM -- Morning workout	9:15 AM - 9:45 AM -- Morning workout
9:45 AM - 10:15 AM -- Daily devotional	9:45 AM - 10:15 AM -- Daily devotional
10:15 AM - 10:45 AM -- Shower/ dress	10:15 AM - 10:45 AM -- Shower/ dress
10:45 AM - 11:30 AM -- Breakfast/ read	10:45 AM - 11:30 AM -- Breakfast/ read
11:30 AM - 1:00 PM -- Do <u>inside</u> work	11:30 AM - 1:00 PM -- Do <u>inside</u> chores
1:00 PM - 4:30 PM -- Visit museums	1:00 PM - 4:30 PM -- Malls/shopping
4:30 PM - 5:15 PM -- Rest/read, audio	4:30 PM - 5:30 PM -- Rest, tea, read/TV
5:15 PM - 5:45 PM -- Tea, read, audio	5:30 PM - 6:15 PM -- Computer, calls
5:45 PM - 6:15 PM -- Computer, calls	6:15 PM - 6:45 PM -- Happy Hour, TV
6:15 PM - 6:45 PM -- Happy Hour, TV	6:45 PM - 7:45 PM -- Dinner (longer ?)
6:45 PM - 7:45 PM -- Dinner (longer ?)	7:45 PM - 8:30 PM -- Chores, music
7:45 PM - 8:30 PM -- Chores, music	8:30 PM - 11:30 PM -- Read, TV, audio
8:30 PM - 11:30 PM -- Read, TV audio	11:30 PM - 12:00 AM -- Read/TV in bed
11:30 PM - 12:00 AM -- Read/TV (bed)	

NOTES: (1) As the chart says, this type schedule is for fall or winter days
with *bad weather days* -- when we really can't get outside and enjoy it. We
looked at our "appealing things list" and drew from the list many of the things
that were mostly inside (museums, shopping centers, art galleries, concerts,
lectures, etc.)

(2) As with the first chart, your own list will no doubt differ from
mine.

Typical Spring or Summer Daily Schedules

Weekday -- Good Weather	Weekday -- Bad Weather
7:00 AM -- 7:30 AM -- Coffee, TV, read	7:00 AM - 7:45 AM -- Coffee, TV, read
7:30 AM - 8:30 AM -- Morning workout	7:45 AM - 8:45 AM -- Morning workout
8:30 AM - 9:00 AM -- Daily devotional	8:45 AM - 9:15 AM -- Daily devotional
9:00 AM - 9:30 AM -- Shower & dress	9:15 AM - 9:45 AM -- Shower & dress
9:30 AM - 9:45 AM -- Breakfast snack	9:45 AM - 10:30 AM -- Breakfast/ read
9:45 AM - 10:15 AM -- Computer work & house chores	10:30 AM - 11:30 AM -- Computer work & house chores
10:15 AM - 1:15 PM -- Get outside -- sports, yard work, walks, hikes, jog, etc.	11:30 AM - 12:00 PM -- Read, light snack (if hungry)
1:15 PM - 2:15 PM -- Light snack, relax	12:00 PM - 3:45 PM -- Sight-seeing, shop
2:15 PM - 2:45 PM --Rest, read, watch TV, listen to music, etc.	3:45 PM - 4:15 PM -- Rest, read, watch TV, listen to music, etc.
2:45 PM - 5:00 PM -- Outside again; stroll/walk in neighborhood/along river	4:15 PM - 4:45 PM -- Afternoon tea, more reading, TV/audio, and relax
5:00 PM - 5:30 PM -- Shower & dress	4:45 PM - 5:30 PM -- Computer, calls
5:30 PM - 6:00 PM -- Tea, read, TV/audio	5:30 PM - 6:00 PM -- Happy Hour, TV
6:00 PM - 6:30 PM -- Computer/mail/ make calls	6:00 PM - 7:00 PM -- Dinner (longer ?)
6:30 PM - 7:00 PM -- Happy Hour, TV	7:00 PM - 8:00 PM -- Chores, music
7:00 PM - 8:00 PM -- Dinner (longer ?)	8:00 PM - 10:30 PM -- Read, TV, audio
8:00 PM - 8:45 PM -- Chores, music	10:30 PM - 11:00 PM -- Read/TV in bed
8:45 PM - 10:45 PM -- Read/TV/audio	
10:45 PM - 11:00 PM -- Read/TV in bed	

NOTES:

(1) In Appendix 2-3 you see a type schedule for those wonderful days of spring and summer; we show both the _good weather days_ and the _bad weather days_. These warmer days let us get outside and do the things we really love and enjoy. We draw heavily on our favorite outdoor things (yard work, gardening, outside sports, etc.), weather permitting.

(2) Note in both cases, we still made time for the daily essentials (exercise, devotionals, etc.); plus, we did everything in a fairly unrushed, evenly paced manner.

(3) Again, your own list will be quite different, depending on your own likes and dislikes. And, treat the scheduled times as approximate; make them to fit your own needs.

* * *

APPENDIX 2-4 (Typical Long Term Planning Monthly Schedule)

Sunday	Monday	Tuesday	Wed.	Thurs.	Friday	Sat.
						1 Yard work
2 Church, weekly Sunday	3	4 Shop or go to Mall	5	6 Work on tennis game	7 Dine with friends in evening	8 Yard work
9 Church, weekly Sunday	10 Work on tennis game	11 Shopping Ctr. or Mall	12 Visit kids	13 Visit kids	14 Visit kids	15 Yard work
16 Church, weekly Sunday	17	18 Shopping Ctr. or Mall	19 Work on tennis game	20 Church work	21 Dine with friends in evening	22 Yard work
23 Church, weekly Sunday	24	25 Shopping Ctr. or Mall	26	27 Work on tennis game	28 Theater in town, evening	29 Yard work
30 Church, weekly Sunday	31 Work on tennis game					

Appendix 2-5 (Long Term Planning -- chart shows how monthly, quarterly, semi-annual and annual events are worked in)

January	February	March
Trip to Hawaii & sun! 10 days to 2 weeks.	Visit Beach Condo Visit Grandchildren	Regional Meeting Theater, evening
April	**May**	**June**
Weekend in Florida/TX Visit Beach Condo	Visit Grandchildren Attend Annual Meeting (Prof. Engineers)	Early visit to Condo Weekend @ Homestead Theater in evening
July	**August**	**September**
Visit Beach Condo Weekend in Mountains	Visit Beach Condo Regional Meeting Visit Grandchildren	Weekend at Greenbriar Visit Beach Condo Theater in evening
October	**November**	**December**
Regional Meeting Visit Europe, 15 days	Visit Beach Condo Visit Grandchildren	Visit Beach Condo Weekend @ Homestead

INDEX

ENDNOTES . . . . .

[1] See Frank L. Schick and Renee Schick, Statistical Handbook on Aging Americans, (Phoenix: Oryx P, 1994) 1.

[2] Census of 1992, Statistical Abstract of the United States, (Washington, D.C.: Dept. of Comm., 1994) 87.

[3] Ibid. 47.

[4] AARP reports their source: the Department of Health and Human Services who defines "in the labor force" as those people who are working or seeking employment.

[5] Frank L. Schick and Renee Schick, 198.

[6] Norman Vincent Peale, The Power of Positive Living, (New York: Doubleday, 1990), 53.

[7] On the subject of retiring, one reference source confirms these statements when it says: "The standard age for retirement has become 65, but many persons who can afford it retire earlier -- at 60 or even 55. Others prefer to stay on the job until they are 70 or older" (Compton's Encyclopedia, 1993 ed.), 178.

[8] My designation of Type A and Type B are not to be confused with the commonly cited A and B personalities which are said to be associated with heart disease.

[9] Norman Vincent Peale, The Power of Positive Thinking, (Edgewood Cliffs, NJ: Prentice Hall, 1956) 66, 69.

[10] Ibid, 76

[11] Junius Ellis, sr. ed., Guide to a Secure Retirement, by ed. of Money Magazine, (Birmingham: Oxmoor Howe, 1989) 38.

[12] Peter A. Dickinson, The Complete Retirement Planning

<u>Book</u>, (New York: E.P. Dutton, 1984) 83.

[13] See Edward L. Palder, <u>The Retirement Sourcebook</u>, (Silver Spring, MD: Woodbine House, 1989) 66-73.

[14] See Hans Selye, <u>The Stress of Life</u> (New York: McGraw-Hill, 1956).

[15] Frederick J. Stare, M.D., and Elizabeth M. Whelan, Sc.D., <u>Eat O.K. -- Feel O.K.</u> (North Quincey, MA: Christopher Publishing, 1978), 192.

[16] Every time my wife and I take a physical exam, the "readings" confirm our excellent physical condition. Our blood pressure, cholesterol, oxygen intake calculations, and all the other critical measurements are right in the "ideal" range. We take *no* medication and don't intend to!

[17] Mary Ellen Pinkham, <u>How to Become a Healthier, Prettier You</u>, (Garden City, NY: Doubleday, 1984) 86.

[18] When you dig deeply into exercising, you will see a lot of puzzling advice. On frequency, for example, if you look into the "every other day" program routine, you might wonder whether this means three or four times a week (there being only seven days in the week). One expert says exercising four times a week is three times as effective as exercising only three times a week. (I am an engineer, and I did not follow that math either!) Anyway, the point is (I think) that we should all get as much exercise during the week as we can handle.

[19] Those who have real, continuing problems sleeping probably need more detailed advice. You definitely should consult the experts. You will find the local libraries and those of the universities loaded with good material. Of course, your local physician (and God) are also at hand.

[20] See the 91st Psalm. The first verse of this favorite reads: "He that dwelleth in the secret place of the most High shall abide under the shadow of the Almighty." Verses 10 and 11 go on to say: "There shall no evil befall thee, neither shall any

plague come nigh thy dwelling. For he shall give his angels charge over thee, to keep thee in all thy ways" (King James version).

[21] This may be putting it too mildly. The standard marathon race is 26 miles and 385 yards. This is the distance between Marathon and Athens -- in Greece -- where the race originated during the first modern Olympic games in 1896. Those of us who have tried running know that long-distance running takes special skills and extreme dedication and training. Only a few attain the level of fitness and determination to make it to the end of a real marathon race.

[22] I have many friends who decided to engage in "part-time" consulting when they retired. If they were good (and most were) and their companies were satisfied (and, again, most were), soon each friend found that their originally agreed upon "few hours" with the firm started to creep upward to whole days, then weeks, and finally, months. Some even found more difficulty in disengaging from these quasi-temporary assignments than in their earlier, life-lone positions. This led to obvious frustration and disenchantment when they found that they had not retired after all.

[23] Dickinson, Retirement Planning, 186.

[24] The reports of some relocation experts can be startling. One says that relocating to certain nearby overseas places will enable living expenses to drop to as little as $400 per month (in certain parts of Mexico and Central America). See John Howells, Retirement Choices (San Francisco: Gateway Books, 1987), 293-314. Another source reports: "...you can rent a retirement home for under $200 a month in Mexico or Costa Rico or buy for another $40,000" (Dickinson, Retirement Planning, 206, 207).

[25] Norman D. Ford, The 50 Healthiest Places to Live and Retire in the United States (New York: Ballentine, 1991),

preface, 11.

[26] Statistical Abstract, 1994, 56.

[27] Schick, Handbook On Aging, 48, 49.

[28] Of course, another possibility is that *both* the man and his spouse will pass on *together*. However, that happens in so few cases that it is rather unlikely.

[29] John Donne.

Notes

Notes

Notes

ORDER FORM

Please send me _____ copies of this book ($9.95 per copy). Mail to:

Name: _____

Address:_____

City:_____ State:_____ Zip:_____

    I am enclosing for the book/s $_____
          (plus)
    Postage & handling* $_____
    Sales tax (where applicable) $_____

    Total amount enclosed $_____

*Please add $3 for the first book and $1 for each additional book.

Send check or money order (no cash or CODs) to:
    Walter O. Bachus
    3808 Great Neck Court
    Alexandria, VA 22309

Prices and numbers subject to change without notice.
Valid only in the U.S.
All orders subject to availability.

For questions or additional information, please call:
    703-360-3607.